MW01132472

Personal Vision

Graham Jones

ISBN: 978-1-964084-00-8

Foreword by Brian Simmons

Author of The Passion Translation

In "Personal Vision," Graham Jones, a pastor, missionary, and author, delves deep into the profound concept of personal vision. This book is a compelling and thought-provoking exploration of one's divine purpose, that invites readers on a transformative journey with God, emphasizing the divine desire for us to understand our true purpose. Graham paints a vivid picture of God's intricate and glorious plan for every aspect of His creation, with a focus on the reader as the pinnacle of His design. He beautifully articulates the idea that no facet of life should be exempt from the influence of God's divine blueprint.

Graham Jones's wisdom and insight shine through every page; This book is not just a read; it's an invitation to embark on a transformative journey with God.

Brian Simmons
Author of The Passion Translation

Acknowledgments

"He who walks with the wise will be wise"
(Proverbs 13:20 NKJV).

I wish to express gratitude to all of the wise individuals with whom I have had, and continue to have, the privilege of walking.

- Harry Greenwood taught me perhaps more than anyone about walking with God, hearing His voice, and living a life of faith. "He, being dead, still speaks" (Hebrews 11:4 NKJV).
- Don Carpenter has taught me about a life of integrity, joy, and the Holy Spirit as a traveling evangelist and missionary.
- Marc & Anne Marie Lebrun are amazing Pastors dedicated to revival in Paris, France. I honor their passion, vision, dedication to mission, and the cause of Christ.
- Brian Simmons was the first pastor I met in the USA who opened the gateway of New England to me. His influence and passion for God have touched the nations.
- Ruth Heflin was a modern day mystic. Her example and message of the glory of God have shaped my understanding of worship.
- Linda Halpert is a lover of God and passionate about God's kingdom and people. It is a privilege to know and work with her.
- To all of my teams, with whom I co-labor in the USA and Europe, it is a joy to walk with you, and I am better for knowing each of you.
- To my beautiful wife Léa Jones, thank you for this journey, all you are in my life, and your example.
- Thanks be to God for His indescribable gift of Jesus Christ. (2 Corinthians 9:15 NKJV)

Introduction

This is not a book of answers; this is a book of questions. This book is an invitation to embark on a journey with God. The God who calls us out of darkness into light desires for us to understand who He is calling us to be.

I love questions. I love questions because Jesus loves questions. Answers are easy; questions are difficult. When God asks us questions, He is not looking for an answer. He already knows the answer; rather, He is inviting us to spend time with Him and fellowship around the question.

- Who are you?
- Who does God call you to be?
- How do others perceive you?
- How do you perceive yourself?
- How does God perceive you?

The two most important things in your life are what you think about God, and what God thinks about you. This book will take you on a journey to clarify those questions. God is a disruptor. He loves to intervene in the lives of His children and change those lives that are off course.

My prayer is that this book will disrupt the course of your life in glorious ways. This book is an invitation to embark on a journey of discovery. This journey will help you both discover and define God's plan for your life and walk with Him.

God has an intricate and glorious plan for every part of His creation. You are the greatest part of that creation. You were designed and intended to live and flourish in a relationship with the most amazing person in the universe. There is no aspect of your life that should be excluded from the influence of God's plan. God is a planner. God is a visionary. God has never done anything by accident, and has never been surprised by anything. He does not live in reaction or response to anything other than His glorious plan.

Everything in heaven and earth is working together for the good of those who submit to and connect with God's plans and purposes for their lives (Romans 8:28). There is no greater calling for our lives than to discover, define, and enter into God's plans. I believe that there is, in heaven, a blueprint of God's perfect vision and plan for your life. The goal of this book is to unveil that vision and bring it to you.

I believe there is a knowledge planted deep in the hearts of every person: that we are on this earth for a purpose. There is, in each of us, a deep longing for significance. In every child born upon the Earth, there is an innate desire to hope and dream. Nobody has ever had to teach a child how to dream. It would appear that God has planted the ability and capacity to dream deep in the heart of every person. The sad reality is that we often teach and train our children not to dream. We mentor them to be realistic, to only engage with the practical realities of life. God is a dreamer, a planner, and a visionary. I believe that through the pages of this book, God is inviting you to reconnect with that inner child, and to dream again.

This world is filled with blind men walking. The Bible says where there is no vision the people perish (or cast off restraint) Prov. 29:18 The world is full of sighted people with no vision. It is filled with emotional vagrants who wander aimlessly without plan or purpose. Someone once asked the famous blind innovator, Helen Keller, if there was anything worse than being blind. Keller immediately replied, 'Yes, to have sight and yet to live without vision.' As an experiment, find a safe and secure environment, perhaps with a friend to assist you. Close your eyes and imagine being blind for the next 10 minutes. Move around an area, even if it is one you are familiar with, without relying on your eyesight. When we experience blindness, our ability to function in the world becomes limited. We become vulnerable to natural hazards and potential attacks. In a state of blindness, we are unaware of the opportunities life presents as we navigate through it. Perhaps most tragically, if we are blind, we miss out on experiencing the beauty and magnificence of life around us. If this holds true for physical blindness, consider how much more profound it could be for those who are spiritually blind to the vision that God has for them.

Nature abhors a vacuum. When we live without a personal vision, we simply default to the vision and values of the world around us. It is vital that we discover the personal plan that God has for our lives and not simply live out a secondhand version of somebody else's vision for us. A person without a vision is a ship without a rudder. A person without a vision is a person without an identity. Our identity is defined and determined by our vision. Without a vision, we cannot see God. Without a vision, we cannot truly see ourselves, or indeed others. The person without a vision will never become the man or woman that God has truly destined them to be. God has designed each and every person to fulfill a specific role in His glorious design for the universe. It is only when we allow the Holy Spirit to unveil the vision He has for us that we can fully enter into that plan and rejoice in it.

Vision releases passion, purpose, and motivation. We have all experienced seasons in our lives when we are overflowing with these things. There are days when we rise with a sense of expectation and anticipation for the present and the future. And yet, there are all too many moments when we feel listless, rudderless, and without direction. In the depths of most people, there is a gnawing sense that they are not living the life that God has intended for them. This void can eat away at them on the inside as they watch the clock of their lives tick by.

This book contains the answers to those challenges. While it will not solve every problem in your life, if you engage with the truths presented here, this book will help you to establish a personal vision and roadmap for your life with God. God desires to move you from living by accident to living on purpose, to move you from the assumed to the defined. There is no greater purpose than fulfilling the destiny and call that God has for your life.

The aim of this book is to serve as a practical tool and guide, aiding you in discovering and defining a personal vision for your life. This book serves to give you a framework around which you can take a season to meet God and 'enquire of the Lord' about His plans and purposes for you. This book will challenge you to reflect and seek God's heart about the main pillars of your spiritual life and then turn those thoughts into a written vision.

We are all guilty, to a greater or lesser degree, of avoidance. It is inherent in our nature to avoid lifting up the foundation stones of our lives and seeing what is truly underneath. God calls us to be circumstantially insecure, and yet relationally secure. At times, we mask that avoidance with busyness or focusing on other areas of our lives. As you journey through this book, allow the Holy Spirit to challenge you to lean not on your own understanding and invite Him and His thoughts into specific areas of your life. We cannot change our past. This book is an invitation to lay the past to rest and to live in the space between the now and the future that God calls you into. To do this, we want to allow God to define and clarify that future in a vision that is clearly accessible to us

In this book, we will explore ten foundational areas of our walk with God. Our goal is to have a written vision for each of these

- The New Creation
- Word of God
- Faith
- Understanding Our Soul
- The Life of Worship
- The Holy Spirit
- Kingdom Finances
- Kingdom Relationships
- Hearing God's Voice & Guidance
- The Disciplines of the Kingdom

Throughout the Bible, God would invite people to leave the past behind and walk with Him into a future that He would define for them, only as they continued that journey with Him

(Hebrews 11:8).

When God called Abraham, His invitation was the following:

I will show you
I will make you
I will bless you

Genesis 12:12

At junctures in our lives, there are moments when God desires to encounter us and shift our perspective. In many instances in the Bible, God would take someone aside, often to an elevated place, and show them the territory He had called them to possess. There is a shift in our thinking when we behold the landscape of our future. When we see our future, we also see our identity. God was speaking to them about the person they would become and the relationship He would build with them on this journey. This book extends an invitation to ascend to a spiritual summit with God. It beckons you to open yourself to God's perspective, igniting your heart with a vision for the comprehensive plans and purposes He has for your life. It invites God to reveal the person He desires to mold, change, and transform you into, enabling you to inherit the promised land He has designated for you.

This book is an invitation to meet God and allow Him to define your life for the now and for the future. It is an opportunity to lay to rest the ghosts of your past and become part of that new generation that will possess the promised land. We will be inquiring of the Lord and asking Him to give a clear, precise, and written vision for each of the most important areas of your life. Certain books in our lives become companions on our life's journey. There are books which seem to demand periodic revisits. Have you ever revisited a book from a previous phase of your life? You may find that the book appears entirely different when read through the lens of your current experiences. Though the book remains unchanged, you have changed and grown.

Come on a journey and allow God to change you.

Chapter One

The Power of A Personal Vision

"For I know the thoughts that I think toward you," says the Lord, "thoughts of peace and not of evil, to give you a future and a hope."
Jeremiah 29:11

"Write the vision
And make it plain on tablets,
That he may run who reads it."
Habakkuk 2:2

Vision is what we see, perceive, and understand. Vision determines our understanding of the future. Vision aligns the dispositions of our hearts as we look towards the future. Our response to vision will determine whether we embrace and run into that future or pull back and hide in the shadow of our fears. Vision determines identity and destiny. Every single thing that God has ever done reveals who God is. Everything that God has ever made or created shines and reflects His beauty and glorious intentionality. God does nothing by accident; he is the ultimate visionary. He sees everything and looks at your life through the lens of vision and hope.

Every plan and vision that we could ever dream for our own life is small, miserable, and insignificant, when compared to the plans that God has for us, both in this life and for eternity. We dream in black and white, whereas the God of the universe dreams in glorious colors, of which we cannot even conceive. God has already seen every part of your life from the moment of your birth until you take your last breath. There is not one thing that you will ever need that God has not foreseen and provided for your life. The saddest thing in humanity is when we turn from God's plan and intention to forming our own. We are not visionaries. We live dull and lackluster lives. We find it hard to see what is right in front of our face.

I have been traveling in ministry since the 1980's. For many years, I have visited churches and conferences all over the world. One of the frustrations of a traveling minister is simply locating the church or hotel that one needs to find. I began traveling in ministry long before the days of the Internet and certainly before the days of GPS. There are many times when I have visited a church that has sent me directions on how to find it. I know that they understood the directions, but when you are traveling in a car at night in an unfamiliar place, it is often very hard to follow such directions. I have visited the nation of Ireland for many years. I love the Irish people dearly, but the country roads of Ireland can be difficult to navigate for one who is not familiar with them. I have literally had people tell me 'to turn left at the tree,' 'to turn right at the cow,' or that I may see a tractor here and need to take the third left after the fence, etc. In the early years of the new millennium, I began traveling in ministry to America. At the time, I would print out traveling directions using MapQuest, a service that would give you a set of directions to follow that would lead you to your destination. There was only one problem with this procedure: it would work as long as you followed every direction perfectly. But the moment that you missed your turn or were on a highway with several choices and missed the right one, then all of the following directions would be worthless. The only hope was to go backward (sometimes several miles) to find the last known place and proceed from there. I am grateful for GPS or a GPS enabled smartphone. The beauty of GPS is found in two things: firstly, that it has an accurate and complete map of the area; secondly, it is able to locate you at any given moment, your direction of travel, and speed, and to marry these two facts together in a way that will help and direct you. When you have a GPS device, it does not matter if you take the wrong turning, which we have all done. A GPS will simply find your current location and plot a dynamic path from where you are to where you need to go. In the same way, God has a plan, map, or vision for our lives. He also has a guide on the inside called the Holy Spirit. In this book, we will explain how to allow God to define the map of your life and how to allow the Spirit of God to interact with that map in a way that will constantly recalibrate you and bring you nearer to God's heart and plan for your life.

God is not merely logical; He is wise. We are connected with a person who knows everything, sees everything, understands everything, and possesses perfect wisdom. God has a map for your life and has placed within you the perfect guide in the person of the Holy Spirit, who can help lead and navigate you through life's journey. The call of Jesus to those first disciples was simply summed up in two words, 'follow me.' It is interesting that the disciples did not respond as rational Western Christians might have. Perhaps Peter would have asked, 'Where are we going?' In response, Jesus would simply smile and say, 'I am not telling you. But put your hand in mine, join me on a journey through this life and the next.' In the same manner, God comes to each and every one of us with the same challenge: 'Follow me.' He invites us to place our hands in His, to learn the daily discipline of leaning not on our own understanding, acknowledging Him in all our ways, and believing that He will direct our paths. (Proverbs 3:56)

To what extent do we determine the decisions of our own lives? How much control do you have over the course of our lives? We often live with the illusion that we control the majority of those decisions. I want to suggest to you that, in fact, the opposite is true. The majority of the decisions we make are determined by forces and influences outside of our control. Christians can talk glibly about the concepts of free will in our lives and the power of choice, yet I want to suggest to you that we delegate most of our choices to others without even being aware of this reality.

This can occur in several ways:

1. Our upbringing determines many of the unconscious choices we make. When we have learned to think or react in a certain way, we are often not even aware of it, and it exerts a massive influence within our lives.

2. Our culture determines much of the vision and direction of our lives. Cultures are determined by the collective memes of thoughts, perspectives, memories, values, and much more, which every member of that cultural group unconsciously assimilates. Culture is the water we swim in, and like a fish, most of us are

not aware of that water. It is interesting when we travel to another culture how often we are aware of the differences that exist in contrast to our own. Often, as visitors, we are aware of things in other people's cultures that they themselves do not see, and the same is true of ourselves. Heaven has a culture; heaven has values. Heaven has a language, and it is the language of promise.

3. We are all influenced by experiences through which we have walked. We have all traversed trauma to some degree. These experiences leave their mark and shape us into the individuals we have become. Having endured particular experiences, we possess an inherent desire to never revisit those moments in our lives. This can engender within us unconscious desires to steer clear of people, situations, and places with which we associate that experience. Often, like a dog with an invisible fence, we live with boundaries that constrain the choices we make in life.

In point of fact, many of us are living our lives based on the agendas and visions of other people. Some of this is conscious, some unconscious, and some rooted in historical reasons. As a Christian, I believe in a real and personal demonic realm that seeks to influence our lives in malevolent ways, leading us away from God.

The goal of this book is to help you transition from living an accident driven life to living a purpose driven one. Essentially, God desires for you to live intentionally. He wants to reveal His purposes to you, for you to embrace them, and to be captivated by His intentions. When we absorb these insights, we become equipped to integrate His purposes seamlessly into the fabric of our daily lives, navigating its ebb and flow with purpose and meaning. When we learn to live on purpose, it is remarkable how many of our life's problems can be solved. As human beings, many of us live with an inherent listlessness. Yet, we were made by the most purposeful Being in the universe and designed with a specific purpose in mind. When you understand your overarching purpose in life, it becomes easier to discern the individual purpose of each day. There is something wonderful about knowing that you are not merely watching your life slip away.

The Bible tells us that David served the purpose of God in his generation, and then he died and went to be with his fathers. (Acts 13:36 NKJV) To what extent are you living out God's purposes in your life right here and right now?

Moreover, living on purpose will also lead to fulfilling relationships with others. People are naturally drawn to and inspired by anyone who knows their purpose in life. Living a life of vision and purpose leads to a fulfilled life. It means living a life that is not easily distracted by life's challenges. Living on purpose enables us to navigate through seasons of attack, hardship, and persecution. Living a life of purpose is living the life that God planned and intended for you. A personal vision means allowing God's vision for our lives to permeate every aspect of our existence. There is tremendous power in having a vision that excites and motivates us in all our endeavors. Having a personal vision can alleviate the lack of motivation that afflicts the average person. When we can see from a high perspective where we are headed and what we will achieve, and when we recognize both the need and God's ability to meet it, a glorious power is released into our lives, changing and motivating us as we walk with God.

* * *

Many of us have a partial vision for some areas of our lives while being completely devoid of vision in others. It is very common, in fact, more the norm than the exception, to encounter individuals who are fervently passionate and motivated about certain aspects of their lives but lack any vision or plan for others. We have all encountered individuals motivated by health, sports, or physical fitness who disregard their intellectual life. Likewise, we have seen people in business driven by money, success, and climbing the corporate ladder, yet lacking vision for their personal lives, families, health, etc. Regrettably, it is all too common in the Christian community to find someone passionate about ministry and building the kingdom of God but lacking vision for personal holiness. God is deeply invested in every area of your life and desires to lead you into a life of wholeness. Just as God instructed the children of Israel to drive out all the inhabitants of the promised land, warning them of the consequences of leaving any tribes behind, He is interested in every area of your life being surrendered to Him. When Joshua led Israel into the promised land, he obeyed God's commands for the most part, yet he left the nation of the Jebusites on Mount Zion in Jerusalem. While Israel possessed the promised land, the Jebusites thrived among them. King David's first act upon becoming king was to drive out the Jebusites. (2 Samuel 5:67 NKJV) As you progress through this book, I urge you not to leave any areas of your life under the brutal occupation of a lack of vision.

For each area of vision we explore, I want you to grasp the emotions and heart of God toward you as His child in that aspect of life. Let us not perceive the will of God as a mere bureaucratic decree but as His desires and wishes. Instead of examining a specific area of our lives and asking, "What is God's will for this?", we should inquire, "How does my Father God desire me to thrive in this area? What are His thoughts and emotions concerning this aspect of my life?" As we delve into each area, ponder and write down what God desires your heart to experience in that domain. Consider how certain areas of our lives evoke joy and hope, instantly putting a smile on our faces. When we think of our children, for instance, we see them through a lens of love, promise, and possibility. This is precisely how God views your life and how He wants you to perceive it.

A vision serves as an invitation to meet God in the midst of that vision. When God gives us a vision, He is not speaking to our innate abilities to accomplish it on our own. When God gives us a vision, He is actually calling us to upgrade our relationship with Him. When God gives us a vision, He is calling us into a new place of relationship with Him that will be required for us to become the person who can accomplish that vision. Generally speaking, God will not give you a vision for things that you can do on your own. God will not give you a vision for things that are easy. God will not give you a vision for things that you have already done many times. God wants to bring us out of self reliance and self dependency into a glorious relationship of reliance and dependency upon Him.

Vision is a royal invitation. A vision is a summons from the king to come to a high place with Jesus. When God gives you a vision, He is not inviting you to strategize about how you can make this happen in your own wisdom and resource. When God gives you a vision, He is inviting you into a place of fellowship with Him. God is interested in relating to us and building an identity with us that is not based on our past but based on His promise. In Genesis 18, the Lord visited Abraham with two angels. He sat down and had a meal of fellowship with Abraham. During this meal, God spoke to Abraham about the child that Abraham and Sarah would have. Sarah was listening to this conversation through the lens of impossibility, through the lens of her own inability to have children. God wanted to fellowship with Abraham around the promise on Abraham's life and God desires to do the same with you and me. At one point during this meal, the Lord said to one of the angels who was present, 'Should I hide from Abraham the thing I am now doing, seeing that Abraham will one day become the father of many nations?' God wishes to relate to us on His promise and not open our past or present identity.

We do not see the word "vision" used often in the New Testament. Rather, the word that is used is "hope." In modern parlance, we have reduced the word "hope" to a very low level word. To the average person, the word holds the significance of a vague desire for something that may possibly, or may not happen in their lives. When the Bible uses the word "hope," it means a completely different concept. Biblical hope indicates a defined, clear, and passionate reality that lives in the heart. When the Bible describes a man possessed by hope, it is not speaking of a fleeting wish or desire. The Bible says that "hope does not disappoint." (Romans 5:5). The Bible speaks of hope as literally an anchor that goes through the veil of the Holy of Holies and is wrapped around the very throne of God (Hebrews 6:19). We use the word hope to express a possible desire or wish, when God speaks of hope, He is speaking about certainty.

Hope is what is seen in the eyes of a bride coming down the aisle of a wedding ceremony to meet the groom. It is not some vague sense that one day, in the distant future, something might happen. It speaks of a promise and it speaks of reality. Hope is what a child has as it goes to bed on Christmas Eve. It is not a sense that possibly sometime in the future its parents may bless it with a gift. Hope is to live in the heart reality and a glorious expectation. "Christ in you, the hope of glory" (Colossians 1:27). God wants to fill your life with glorious hope. God wants you to be literally possessed by hope. In recent years, we have heard much good and valid teaching about faith. Some have often struggled to realize or understand why that teaching on faith has not produced results in their lives. I want to suggest to you that one of the problems is not a lack of faith, but rather a lack of hope. Hebrews 11:1 says that faith is the substance of things hoped for. If we do not have real Bible hope dwelling in our hearts, our faith will not produce anything. I have discovered that the person with the most hope in any given situation will be the person with the most influence. Hope releases the influence of heaven upon our lives. There is a language in heaven. It is not English, it is not French, it is not Hebrew, and it may not even be speaking in tongues. The language of heaven is the language of promise. The language of heaven is the language of hope and possibility. God wants to teach us this language. God wants us to speak this language, and we learn the language of hope as we begin to allow the Holy Spirit to write down His vision, both on paper and, more importantly, on the tablets of our hearts. (Romans 15:13 NKJV)

When God shows a vision to us, He is not describing us; rather, He is creating us. God is not interested in describing us in our current state, only when He requires us to change and repent. Rather, when God speaks to us, His very word contains within it the power to change and become the person He is describing. In

Judges chapter 6, we read the story of Gideon. God's address to Gideon through the angel is "The Lord is with you, you mighty man of valor." (Judges 6:12 NKJV). There is not one person alive in Israel, at that juncture, who would have described Gideon as a mighty man of valor. There was nothing mighty or valorous about Gideon. After hearing from God, Gideon went to the center of his village, and pulled down a Satanic idol which had been there for a long time. Nothing whatsoever had changed in the nation of Israel, but something has changed in Gideon's own heart, in Gideon's own perception of himself. Everybody is a mighty man of valor when God is with them.

God has things to declare over your life. The goal of vision is to take these words, promises, and proclamations of God and turn them into pictures of hope that we can look upon and allow them to change us. Our heart has the power to enable us to see the unseen. "Faith is the evidence of things unseen" (Hebrews 11:1 NKJV). Faith will take the unseen things of hope and bring them into the seen world of our lives. It is vital that we realize the creative nature of God's word. Hebrews 11:3 says, by God's word, God created the heavens and the Earth. It is the power of God's word that will create the plans and purposes that God has for you. When we look upon a vision, we see things as God already sees them in eternity. There is a place in God where we look less upon ourselves, less upon what we can see, and our gaze is fixed on the thing that God has shown us.

"By faith [Moses] endured as seeing Him who is invisible" (Hebrews 11:27 NKJV).

Chapter Two

Defining Our Vision

In this chapter, we will explore practical ways to use this book and allow God to set out a personal vision for your life.

When we speak about vision, we are referring to God's plans, thoughts, and intentionality toward you as His child. It is vital that we learn to align God's plan and thoughts with our own. God has already affirmed His plan for your life. He desires for you to see His plan and echo your agreement with His. The Lord wants to yoke your thinking and intentionality to His. He has already said yes, and meant it to you; now, He is calling you to say yes, and mean it to Him. (2 Corinthians 1:20 NKJV)

There are specific steps that will aid you as you journey through this book. I encourage you to get a notepad and a pen, preferably a journal or something in which you can jot down personal thoughts and reflections as you progress through this book. I believe there is something powerful, and indeed divine, about the act of writing. Lord Bacon once said, "Writing makes an exact man." God chose the act of writing to communicate with humanity. There is a wonderful lesson we can learn. Writing endures. When we set something down in writing, though the world may change and our emotions may fluctuate, we can always return to that written text. There are times in our lives when we engage passionately with vision, and other times when we lack clarity or motivation about the direction of our lives. We can learn the daily discipline of journaling with God, of capturing His thoughts and making them specific to our lives.

I encourage you to set aside a specific time to engage with this book and allow the Holy Spirit to speak and build this personal vision in your life. I believe it would be worthwhile to commit to having a defined time to work on this process. Perhaps you could read a chapter every morning as part of your devotional time with God. You could study this book with others or as part of a church Bible study. Having a designated time for engaging with this material will motivate you and keep you accountable as you progress. I encourage you to approach this journey systematically, whether day by day or week by week. If you engage with this material sporadically, it will yield ineffective and sporadic results in your life. Approach the subject with the same intentionality and passion that God does. I encourage you to set aside a brief season of your life and ascend to a mountaintop with God, allowing Him to reveal things that may change the direction of your life. It might be appropriate to take a few days off from your work to go away alone and spend time with God on this subject.

The purpose of this book is to provide a framework and vision for some of the most important areas of your life. We need a new wineskin in our thinking, a flexible mindset that can adapt to the current realities. The aim of this book is to help you articulate a personal vision that can evolve, that God can shape over time, yet will remain constant in its values throughout your life. The goal of this book is to empower you to document a vision for each of these areas. As you embark on this journey, I encourage you to commit your way to the Lord. There is something powerful about commitment. When we make a quality decision to commit to something before the Lord, I believe He will honor that commitment and enable us to fulfill and maintain it throughout our lives. (Proverbs 16:3 NKJV)

God will only share His treasures with those who will treasure them. When we commit to God regarding a certain subject, He will unveil His secrets and insights concerning that matter. When we approach God with a serious commitment to seek out His will and ways for our lives, committing to the Lord becomes an act of our will and volition. I believe it is beneficial to renew that commitment before God each and every day. There can be times when all of us fear commitment. It is sometimes easier to live with a vague sense that something needs to change, and it can be disconcerting to actually take the time to examine that area, seek God, and write down your thoughts. Often, like a storage area in our home that we internally resist engaging with, we can have ideas, dreams, thoughts, and fears that we are afraid of bringing into the light. I encourage you to confront those areas of your life honestly and with courage. There is nothing to fear but fear itself. God has already affirmed His plans, promises, and strategies for your life. Every day, as you embark on this journey of uncovering and unveiling this vision for your life, renew your commitment to say yes to God, and He will affirm it.

Our objective in crafting a personal vision is not solely to compile a set of ideas and words. The Holy Spirit functions as an artist, and your heart serves as the canvas upon which He paints.

Our goal in this endeavor is to beseech the Lord to depict a picture, to craft an image that you can perceive, contemplate, and delve into. An image evokes emotions in the beholder. Regarding the ten areas addressed in this book, our aspiration is that God would shape an image that would dwell within you, becoming more tangible than the world you perceive. (John 3:16)

When we discuss vision, we are referring to God reshaping the reality of the world around us to align with the internal reality of His promise. As you progress through the process outlined in this book, permit the Holy Spirit to remove certain images that may currently occupy the canvas of your heart and replace them with those from His heart. God speaks so that we may see. To a greater or lesser extent, we all rely on visual imagery. If I mention the word "dog" to you, it's likely that the letters DOG are not visualized on the screen of your mind. Rather, especially if you're a dog owner like myself, you visualize an actual dog. (Genesis 1:1) If you were to take a moment to gaze upon a picture or design, it is indeed possible to comprehend the entire picture in a moment. It is also possible to zoom in and analyze different parts of that picture, to refine and increase the resolution of your gaze as you engage with it. I believe that God desires to provide us with an image for the significant areas of our lives that we can both summarize effectively and be emotionally moved by in an instant, but also areas that we can spend months scrutinizing in detail, unpacking, analyzing, and praying over.

One of the greatest keys that will aid you in navigating through this process is to grant yourself permission to engage in an imperfect manner. In fact, I urge you to allow yourself to do this poorly! There is power and life in learning to do things poorly, at least initially. We all must learn to produce a subpar first draft. Often, we reside with an internal dialogue that dictates unless we can execute something flawlessly on the first attempt, we should abstain from trying. While this sentiment holds some truth, it is particularly valid when we embark on something of personal value. There exists an internal, subconscious resistance to addressing the significant matters in life. One of the methods we employ to tackle this resistance is a form of procrastination that habitually postpones the important task into the future. Whenever we endeavor to undertake any process with precision and accuracy, we engage the left hemisphere of our brain. This hemisphere is accountable for meticulous attention to detail, error detection, and similar tasks. However, the challenge emerges when we endeavor to nurture creativity, imagination, and uninhibited internal dialogue, as this necessitates the dominance of our right brain.

The art of brainstorming wields remarkable power. Through brainstorming, we afford ourselves the freedom to jot down ideas, even those that may seem flawed. If we withhold permission to record thoughts that might be discarded later, a part of us clings too tightly to the creative process. I urge you to embark on the journey of crafting a personal vision and grant yourself the liberty to document ideas that you might eventually discard. There's no obligation for anyone else to see your writings or thoughts unless you decide to share them. Reconnect with your inner child; rediscover the joy of exploration and play. Allow your imagination to roam freely, inviting the Holy Spirit to infuse it, without concern for external judgment. This lesson is profoundly important across all facets of life, particularly in creative pursuits.

* * *

The kingdom of God operates on relational principles. Everything within God's kingdom functions through the principle of relationship. Religion emerges when we extract the principles of God from the context of a relationship with Him. As you progress through the chapters of this book, I encourage you to scrutinize all these different themes through the lens of relationship. In the forthcoming chapters, we will explore 10 foundational pillars that support your spiritual life and home. I encourage you to contemplate these truths through the lens of relationship:

- What would it resemble to cultivate a new relationship with God in this area of your life?

- What would it resemble to cultivate a new relationship with yourself in this area of your life?

- How would a fresh vision in this area of your spiritual life influence your relationships with other people?

- How do you perceive this truth in your own heart?

When God extends an invitation for you to embark on a journey, He is less concerned about the destination and more focused on the process. When we journey with God, we are entering into a process of transformation. God guided the children of Israel through the wilderness to effect change and transformation within them. As you traverse through the journey outlined in this book, I urge you to perceive it as an opportunity to enhance your walk and relationship with the Holy Spirit. God desires to commune with you, converse with you, encounter you, and effect change and transformation within you.

* * *

I firmly believe that in the last days, all ministry will emanate from relationship. The depth of our ministry will be determined by the depth of our relationship. For God to lead us further and deeper into the marketplace, He must beckon us further and deeper into the secret place. Each of the subsequent chapters presents an invitation to dig wells in the secret place of your heart. The time you invest in this process will yield dividends and yield fountains of living water for the rest of your life.

The key to understanding the old covenant is encapsulated in the word obedience. God would speak to the people of Israel, and all He was seeking from them was obedience. When the people obeyed, the blessings of God would follow. When the people of God disobeyed, they would not be blessed.

The key to understanding the new covenant is wrapped up in the word identity. God is not primarily dealing with His children based on their actions, but rather on their identity. In the old covenant, your actions or performance would determine your identity. You would be considered a good person if you did or performed good things. In the new covenant, your identity determines your performance. You are not good because you do good things. The God of the universe has declared you to be good in Christ Jesus, and as you begin to believe this by faith, you will indeed bear good fruit and do good things. As we walk through the following chapters of this book, it is important to realize that God wants to define vision so that He can rewrite and define your identity. The key to having a personal vision is not to come up with a list of things that we need to do in each of these areas. Rather, it is to allow God to define what our identity is, who we are in our relationship to Him in each of these areas.

One of my favorite books in the Bible is the Book of Joshua. Joshua is a book of vision, victory, and inheritance. Moses is the man who brings the people of Israel out of captivity, but it is Joshua who leads them into the inheritance of the promised land. The first verse in the Book of Joshua reads, "Moses my servant is dead; now arise, and go over this Jordan." (Joshua 1:2) There are times and seasons in our lives when God needs to declare to us that the past is dead. If we are to be the people that God destined us to be, if we are to step into the vision and inheritance that God has for us, we must allow God to declare that the past is truly dead. We cannot drag our yesterdays into our tomorrows. As you walk through this journey, I encourage you to lay to rest your past; to lay to rest your old thinking.

It is time to let go of memories, failures, and hurts from the past. The Bible declares several times that the present and the future belong to us (Psalm 118:24). It is a really important truth to realize, but your past does not belong to you. It is time to forsake the hope of obtaining a better past. One of the keys to life in the spirit is learning to hand your past over to God and not allowing it to influence you as you move forward.

It is vital as we go through the process of defining a personal vision that we do not allow our past failures to determine what is or what is not possible for us in the future. It is vital that our personal vision is based on God's promises and ability alone. We cannot build on the sinking sand of our past. (Matthew 7:2427)

It is important that we forgive from our hearts everybody who has ever hurt us in our past. To a greater or lesser degree, we are all victims. We can all look back at our yesterdays and claim with good cause that life was not fair to us, and that we have been the victims of others. This is true for every person who has ever lived. The first words out of Adam's mouth, after the fall, were to blame his wife. I'm not minimizing or excusing the very real hurt that may have been done to you through others, but I am challenging you to lay this to rest. I am encouraging you not to allow this to become your identity but rather to allow God to define your identity through His promises. Lastly, it is really important that we receive God's forgiveness for our past and that we actually accept and forgive ourselves.

Philippians 3:1214: "Not that I have already attained, or am already perfected; but I press on, that I may lay hold of that for which Christ Jesus has also laid hold of me. Brethren, I do not count myself to have apprehended; but one thing I do, forgetting those things which are behind and reaching forward to those things which are ahead, I press toward the goal for the prize of the upward call of God in Christ Jesus."

I encourage you, as you embark on this journey, to let go of the past, to release yesterday, to recognize that Moses is dead, and now God is summoning you to enter into your promised land. One of the greatest breakthroughs I have ever experienced in this area is learning that the key to laying things to rest is to do so by faith. Most of us do not realize the role that emotions play in our lives. We believe we have forgiven somebody when we feel that we have forgiven them. We believe that God has forgiven us when we feel forgiven. We believe that the past is put to rest when it no longer affects our emotions. The greatest key I know in this area is the key of faith. Faith brings closure to these areas. We can pray and forgive somebody else, and then believe by faith that they are forgiven. We do not base this on our current emotional state, which changes so easily, but rather solely on the promises of God.

Practical steps in writing, thinking and meditation.

Here are some practical steps that will assist you as you progress through the process of writing a personal vision. It is not necessary to complete all of these steps, but I encourage you to revisit this list and allow each item to inform how you engage with this process. For each of the ten area in this book, I encourage you to write a description of your walk with God in this area: For each area, write a brief description of how you want to live for the rest of your life. Frame this description in the present continuous tense, not in an aspirational future sense. For example, "I am walking with God. I have victory every day. I enjoy fellowshipping and walking in a place of constant worship."

Pen and Paper
I encourage you to acquire a private personal journal and jot down your thoughts as you continue through this book. Writing is invaluable as it helps us articulate our thoughts and preserve them for the future.

Commitment:
God honors commitment. You will receive revelation and transformation from this book to the extent that you commit to this process. I urge you, at the outset of this book, to commit wholeheartedly to working through these chapters and engaging fully with this process. As you commit fully to God, He will commit fully to you.

* * *

Group Study:
It may be beneficial to engage in this process as part of a group study. Consider undertaking this with a circle of friends, or as part of a church, Bible study, or small group.

Draft Process:
Give yourself permission to initially approach this imperfectly. The objective is not perfection but rather engagement. As you engage, God will assist you in refining and enhancing your vision. Write down between 10 to 20 thoughts in each chapter that resonate with you and may become pieces of the puzzle in constructing the vision with God.

The Key of Faith:
As you progress through this process, issues from your past may resurface in your heart. Learn to lay the past to rest through faith and believe that it is resolved. If necessary, draft a written agreement with God, laying to rest those past issues. When you encounter challenges in this area, revisit this agreement before God, and thank Him by faith for its accomplishment.

Time Frames:
Learn to view each of the following areas within different time frames. Each aspect of our personal vision can apply to us in the short term, such as the next 30 minutes, and equally apply as we look over the horizon of the next 30 years. Periodically review the previous chapters and your journal entries from each of these time frames. Sometimes, after several days, we perceive things differently, and the scope of our revelation has expanded.

Bible Verses:

Write a list of 5 to 10 biblical declarations that you can memorize and make your own.

Chapter Three

The New Creation

Behold, I make all things new. (Revelation 21:5)

The goal of religion is reformation. The goal of Christianity is transformation. Jesus did not come to reform, patch up, improve, or help you live a better life. Jesus did not come to make bad people into good people. Jesus came to make dead people into alive people.

We begin with the subject of the new creation because this is the most important area of your life. This is actually the beginning and the end of your Christian life. Everything in Christianity centers around this subject, and yet the vast majority of Christians live without any understanding, revelation, or experience of it. If we do not understand this subject, we will live miserable, defeated Christian lives. Without an understanding or revelation of this subject, we are constantly trying in our own strength to become the people that God already sees.

One of the greatest keys to the Christian life is understanding that much of the New Testament is written in the past tense. When the apostles are writing and describing our Christian life, you will see again and again the use of the past accomplished tense.

"He has raised us and seated us in heavenly places in Christ Jesus" (Ephesians 2:6).

"By his stripes, you were healed.

"You have been delivered from the power of the enemy.

You have all things." (1 Peter 2:24, Colossians 1:13, Ephesians 1:3).

The crux of the Christian life lies in understanding that Jesus has already accomplished everything on the cross of Calvary. In Matthew 19:30, Jesus cried out, "It is finished," and at that point, all things needed for your salvation were signed, sealed, and delivered in the blood of Jesus. Religion is working towards a goal of improvement. Christianity is working from the finished work of Jesus. So often, we may find ourselves praying and seeking God, and asking Him to do things that His Word declares are already done. When we pray prayers asking for something, but God has already done it, we are actually praying a prayer that God cannot answer.

In spite of this being a true description of prayer. Often in religion, we find joy in the form of prayer rather than the breakthrough of experiential answers in our lives. God wants to answer our prayers. God wants to give us glorious breakthrough experiences. Jesus said, "Ask and you shall receive, that your joy may be full" (John 16:24). When we pray prayers asking for things that we already have, we deny ourselves the joy of breakthrough and instead find joy in the form of prayer. This is the genesis of religion – a form of godliness denying the power (2 Timothy 3:5).

When we were born again, God placed us into Christ Jesus. There is nothing we need to do to attain this position, or no work needed to maintain this position. We are in Christ. One of the greatest keys to reading the New Testament is to notice the phrases in Christ, "in Jesus", "in him", "in whom", etc. These are a description of our current identity in Christ Jesus. It is so important that we settle this truth within our hearts that we have arrived in Christ Jesus.

I was born in the United Kingdom and hence I am a British citizen. Several years ago having lived in the United States for over 10 years, my wife and I became American citizens. After completing a short ceremony and making a pledge in front of a legal representative, we were declared to be American citizens. I may not look American. I may not sound American. I prefer strong tea to coffee and still like to drive on the correct (left) side of the road. I do not always feel American, and it is quite possible that I do not always act in an American way, and yet, in spite of this, I am an American citizen. I am just as American as any other citizen of that great nation. In the same way, we have been declared to be citizens of Heaven and children of God. God has placed us in Christ Jesus. We have been given an identity that is not based upon our performance. It is based on God's declaration towards us.

It is important we understand that God has nothing to say to our old identity. God is not interested in building a relationship with you in the person you used to be. Everything God wants to do in and through your life will flow through that identity as a brand new creature in Jesus Christ. We must learn to think as new creations.

- We must learn to walk as new creations.
- We must learn to worship as new creations.
- We must learn to relate to God as brand new creations.
- We must learn to relate to ourselves as new creations.
- This is a key to everything in the Christian life.

I believe the most important prayer contained in the whole Bible is the prayer of Paul in Ephesians chapter 1:1622

"I do not cease to give thanks for you, making mention of you in my prayers: 17 that the God of our Lord Jesus Christ, the Father of glory, may give to you the spirit of wisdom and revelation in the knowledge of Him, 18 the eyes of your understanding being enlightened; that you may know what is the hope of His calling, what are the riches of the glory of His inheritance in the saints, 19 and what is the exceeding greatness of His power toward us who believe, according to the working of His mighty power 20 which He worked in Christ when He raised Him from the dead and seated Him at His right hand in the heavenly places, 21 far above all principality and power and might and dominion, and every name that is named, not only in this age but also in that which is to come. And He put all things under His feet, and gave Him to be head over all things to the church, 23 which is His body, the fullness of Him who fills all in all."

In this, Paul's basic request is that God would open the eyes of our understanding, the eyes of our heart, the eyes of our inner man. Paul prays that God would give us wisdom and revelation concerning who we already are in Jesus Christ. Paul continues to say that when we have revelation of this truth, it will fill us with hope (or vision), it will release unto us the inheritance that is ours in Christ Jesus, and finally, God's power will be manifest through our lives. I would challenge you to take this prayer of the apostle Paul's and pray daily over your own life in the first person.

Many people struggle with the concept of how to build a relationship with God. Having spoken to thousands of Christians over the years, I would surmise the vast majority of believers live with a sinking feeling that their relationship with God is not as it should be. Most people who are truly born again know that they love God; in their mind, they know, at least at an intellectual level, that God loves them, but they usually feel distant from God. Most Christians live with an internal sense of guilt and failure concerning their relationship with God. I have had many people say to me over the years, "How do I actually build a relationship with God? I know I am a Christian, but where do I actually begin? What do I need to do to begin to fellowship with him in a real experiential way?"

It is such a glorious realization to understand that we do not have to build a relationship with God. God is not seeking for you to construct a personal relationship with Him. Rather, God is inviting you into a preexisting relationship that He has with His son. I do not possess my own relationship with God. I am in Christ Jesus. To be in Christ Jesus means to literally be in Jesus's relationship with the Father and the Holy Spirit. To enjoy and flourish in that relationship only truly requires three things:

Firstly, we must acknowledge that we have been placed in this relationship. It is beneficial to read this in the pages of the

Bible, or a book such as this, but it is equally important to have the Holy Spirit reveal this truth to our hearts.

Secondly, we must repent from sin and the consciousness of sin. Sin separates us from God. When the believer allows sin to enter into his life, it does not break our relationship with God, but it does alter and affect our fellowship with God. There is a glorious power in turning from oneself, and not attempting to conceal it, but turning to the living God in repentance and asking Him to cleanse you.

The key to flourishing in this relationship is simply to enjoy it. When I am striving and seeking to attain something I already have, that is an acknowledgment that I do not believe I already have it. I was married nearly 25 years ago, that means I am still married. Imagine every day if I was thinking of how I could attain the state of marriage, asking myself if I was still accepted in marriage? We need to learn the glorious daily discipline of enjoying our relationship with God. To do that, we acknowledge the reality that we have arrived, and we have it. We are seated in heavenly places. To be seated carries the idea that there is no more work to be done. Everything is finished and accomplished in Christ Jesus. If we would begin every day with the realization that we have completely arrived, we have nothing left to do, to attain, to add to our Christian relationship, a smile of joy would break out upon our face. We would realize that we have become accepted in the beloved. We are joined with God in Christ, and we are engaged in the lifestyle of enjoying our placement in Christ Jesus.

The communication of your faith is made effective by the constant recognition of everything which you already have in Christ Jesus. (Philippians 1:6).

The new life is designed to fit perfectly with the new creation. It is only the new creation that can step into this new life that God has planned purposefully for us. The new creation fits perfectly into the new life. The new creation has the very nature of God on the inside of him. It is the new creation that can breathe the atmosphere of heaven. The new creation lives in a place of victory as an overcomer in Christ Jesus. You are a perfect fit for the life that God has called you to. The reason we struggle to fit into this new Christian life is that we are trying to do it with an old identity. Religion is concerned with the reformation of the old man. God does not want to change or improve your old man. God's answer for the old man is the crucifixion at the cross of Calvary. You have already been set free from everything in the old. In this chapter, we will explain how.

The revelation of our identity in Christ is the key that will unlock the door into a new life of victory over sin. God does not want to help you try to become a better version of yourself. God does not want to help you manage your sin. Do you understand our placement in Christ? It is vital. But do we understand what really took place upon the cross of Calvary? When Jesus died upon the cross, most of us have been taught that God placed upon Jesus the sins of the world. What does that actually mean? I think most people would say that this means that every sin that has ever been committed, Jesus took upon himself and paid the price to satisfy the justice of God. Let me challenge you today that the finished work of Christ on Calvary was so much bigger than this. I would suggest to you that the major problem that stood between God and man was not actually individual sins or acts that men and women have committed in their lives. Did Jesus die for the lie that was told, the money that was stolen, the adulterous affair, the murder, that has taken place? A resounding yes to all of these things, and yet at the heart of the matter, sin is an identity issue.

Jesus said that when the Spirit of truth has come, He will convict the world of sin. (John 16:8). Sin in the singular, not sins. Jesus paid the price for individual sin. Jesus also paid the price for the very identity and nature of fallen man, the sinful nature. In addition to this, the Bible clearly says that Jesus took upon Himself the sins of the world. That when Jesus died, our old man, our old nature was crucified with Him (Romans 6, Colossians 3). God is not asking you to work on eliminating your old nature, your old man as Paul calls him in Romans. Rather, God has already completely dealt with the nature of sin on Calvary's cross. This is a fact in the mind of God, even if it is not yet the fact in the experience of the average believer.

We must settle this fact in our heart: when Jesus died, we died. (Colossians 3:3). The Bible declares that your old man is absolutely dead. There is a revelation about water baptism that I believe most of us have completely missed. Many of us were taught about water baptism, and often the teaching seems to imply that the purpose of baptism was an induction service about joining the church. Often water baptism is presented as a public decoration of one's faith in Jesus to be made before family and friends. While these ideas might have some minor truths in them, they are actually not remotely biblical.

Simply put, water baptism is one thing. It is a burial service. Water baptism is God's answer to removing your old man. The Bible says when Jesus died upon the cross, our old nature was crucified with him. See this is a fact: when Jesus died, he was then buried. When we were baptized in water, our old man was buried with him in baptism and raised in newness of life. This is not simply a symbolic ceremony. Something actually happens spiritually when one is baptized in water, but it is important that we teach people this reality and also teach them to learn to use what happened in the water to anchor their faith in that reality.

"How shall we who died to sin live any longer in it? Or do you not know that as many of us as were baptized into Christ Jesus were baptized into His death? Therefore we were buried with Him through baptism into death, that just as Christ was raised from the dead by the glory of the Father, even so we also should walk in newness of life." (Romans 6:24).

How do we apply these truths practically in our day-today walk with God? I encourage you to read the whole chapter of Romans six. Probably more than any other chapter in the Bible, this chapter sets out how a believer can step into the fullness of the new creation and live a separate life from the nature of sin. In this passage, Paul encourages the believer to reckon themselves dead to sin and alive to God, to be buried in baptism, and raised in newness of life. This is an act of faith based on God's word, and not based on a human experience. Take a moment to declare these things:

- I am a new creation. All things have passed away and in my life all things have been made new. (2 Corinthians 5:17)
- I am a part of God's divine nature. (2 Peter 1:4)
- My old nature was crucified with Christ. It is no longer I who live but Christ who lives in me. (Galatians 2:20)
- My old man was buried in the water in baptism with Christ, and I am now raised in newness of life. (Romans 6:4)
- I am now seated in heavenly places in Christ Jesus. (Ephesians 2:6)
- I am complete in Jesus. (Colossians 2:10)

If these things are true, as the Bible clearly states, then why is it that the average believer does not experience these things? What is the part, if any, that we need to play in living out the Christian life? One could legitimately pose the question: if these things are true, then we have nothing to do, everything is done. Let me go back to my analogy of becoming a citizen of a new nation. In a single day, I became an American citizen. I received American citizenship. I was fully and absolutely a citizen of America. Is that the only part of my new life in America? No, now the challenge from my perspective is to learn to live out this new life. The challenge from my perspective is to learn to live in a new kingdom, to learn to live with new laws. So, my challenge is to learn to think American, talk American, drive American, eat American, put on the mindset and culture of another nature. My identity was changed in one day, but there is a learning to live in and live out of this new life, that is a process, that will continue all the days of my life. There is probably always a part of me that will need to remind myself I am no longer British. My identity is changed. I am not working for my citizenship by reminding myself of these things. Rather, I am working out my citizenship. I am learning to live as a new citizen in a new realm with a brand new life.

Romans 12:2 "And do not be conformed to this world, but be transformed by the renewing of your mind, that you may prove what is that good and acceptable and perfect will of God."

Ephesians 4:2324 "And be renewed in the spirit of your mind, and that you put on the new man which was created according to God, in true righteousness and holiness."

In order to live out a clear vision of our identity in Christ, we must engage with the following steps:

Firstly, We must spend time to uncover and discover what the Bible clearly says is our identity in Christ. I have included a list of scriptures at the end of this chapter to meditate upon. Take the time to make your own personal list of scriptures, rather than simply copying a generic list. As you read through the Bible on your own, when God highlights part of your identity, add it to that list of verses. It can be a good discipline to write down the entirety of the verse and also the reference and learn them by heart.

Secondly, we need to take time to seek God for revelation about these verses. The secret things belong to the Lord our God, but the revealed things belong to us. It is not enough to fill our minds with biblical truths; it takes an action of the Holy Spirit to write these truths upon the tablet of our heart and give us revelation concerning them. We do this by bringing them to God in prayer. By allowing the Holy Spirit to speak that verse into our heart, and meeting the Lord in the midst of the truth of his word. Learning to speak God's word out loud is a powerful way to bring truth from your mind into your heart. Write down your own vision of who you are in Jesus Christ. The general truths apply to all believers, but God also has individual and personal promises and descriptions that he wishes to declare over you. Engage in the discipline of coming to the Lord and saying, "Lord, show me who I am."

Lastly, develop a vision of what it means for you to live out your identity in your daily life, in the world around you, and in whatever realm of ministry God has called you to. Remember that our identity is the key to our inheritance. Our true ministry is simply the overflow of our relationship with God.

Write down your vision, a description of who God declares you to be. Come back to this often, revisit it, allow the Holy Spirit to expand it, and add to these truths over time. Let this image live big upon you. Come every day to the mirror of God's word, and allow God to show you what you really look like, and then go live that life out each and every day. (Ephesians 1:1718).

Questions for Meditation

- *Are there ideas and scripts about this area of your life that heaven wants to rewrite in this season?*

- *What are the challenges you have in relation to this subject? Describe them as past, defeated, and nailed to the cross.*

- *What is the Lord displacing in your life? What new thing does He want to replace the old with?*

- *How does God define my identity?*

- *Describe the relationship that God is calling you to have with Him in this area.*

- *If God were saying "Yes and Amen", what would your request be?*

- *What would living in complete freedom, joy, and victory look like?*

- *What promise is God speaking over you in this season? What are the promises He is calling you to declare back to Him?*

- *What would transformation look like under your present circumstances?*

- *What would it take for you to develop a mindset, a lifestyle, a persona of fullness as a way of life?*

- *How are you called to minister to others?*

Chapter Four

The Word of God

In this chapter, we will explore developing a personal vision around the daily discipline of engaging with the Word of God. It is important to understand that the life of a Christian is based on two primary things: the Word of God and the Spirit of God. Without engaging our hearts in both of these realities, our relationship with God is theoretical and vague. We engage in a vital, real-life relationship with God by His Spirit, and yet it is important to realize that this is subjective to each and every one of us. When we talk about being led by the Spirit, hearing God's voice, experiencing God, we must embrace the personal subjectivity of these experiences. When we talk about basing our lives upon the written Word of God, we are dealing with something that is absolutely objective, not subject to the whims of how we may be feeling or experiencing. For us to be balanced people, and indeed biblical people, we need both of these realities in our lives.

On the day of Pentecost, God poured out His Spirit on all flesh. For the first time in human history, at least to this degree, a large body of people were having a subjective experience with God that was both real and could be judged by others. The 120 gathered in the upper room saw fire descend upon them, heard themselves and others speaking in other tongues, and heard the sound of a mighty rushing wind. Observers reacted to their behavior and came away with the commentary that they were drunk. This was all experiential. When Peter stood up to preach, he connected the experience that they just had with the written Word of God. Peter addressed the crowd and said, "This is what was spoken by the prophet Joel" (Acts 2:16). This is that. This subjective experience that you see and hear is in line with the written Word of God, which is objectively recognized as the Word of God spoken by the prophet Joel.

We need to be a people of both "this" and "that". We need to be a people of biblical knowledge but also of experiential truth and connect the two together.

In this chapter, I wish to ask some foundational questions about the Word of God. I encourage you to think and reflect, and allow us to shake your viewpoint on what the Word of God actually is.

- What is the Word of God?
- Who is the Word of God?
- What was Jesus's relationship with the written Word of God?
- What should our relationship with the written Word of God be?
- Is the Bible more than a book about God?
- Does God's written Word contain God?

Will the real Word of God stand up? Who or what is the Word of God? We have tended in our modern Christianity to look at the Bible as if it were the operating instructions for the Christian life. Most of us are accustomed to buying electronic devices, and usually within the package of these devices are a set of written instructions for correct usage. I think we often approach the Bible in this way. Some of our modern frustrations with the Bible arise from it not being written in this way, and that when most of us come looking for the "Quickstart guide" to the Christian life, it can feel as if we are wading through genealogies and texts that may seem to have little relevance to our own lives.

One of the greatest revelations we can ever receive as a Christian is when we learn to look at God's words through a completely different lens. Simply put, God's Word is God speaking to us. Take the time to think this through. There would be no difference whatsoever between Jesus appearing in your room right now, shining with all of his glory, and speaking directly to you. Or simply, you opening the words of the Bible, and reading them out loud. God's Word is God's Word, when we begin to realize this, our whole approach and understanding of the written Word of God will change. I believe that most of us, whether we are aware of this or not, are guilty of placing the Bible in a lower category than we would of the person of Jesus. We have placed Jesus on a pedestal as the ultimate Word of God, and we give the Bible, God's written Word, a much lower place in our value and estimation. While we might never intrinsically say or claim that the Bible is not the Word of God, we do not accord it the same honor and expectation that we would if Jesus appeared to us. Right now at this moment, if Jesus walked through the wall of the room you were in and spoke to you, there is a good possibility you would remember those words for the rest of your life. I want to humbly suggest to you that every single word in your Bible has the same power, the same virtue, the same integrity in the eyes of God as Jesus speaking to you. So God's Word is God speaking. God's Word is Jesus. God's Word is also the written Word of God that we have in the book that we call the Bible. There is no difference, no separation in any way, shape, or form between these realities. When we begin to approach the written Word of God in the same way we would approach the reality of God speaking to us, our whole life can be changed and transformed. Anytime that God speaks, that is the Word of God.

God has spoken in various and sundry ways; He has in these last days spoken to us by His Son, who has made the heir of all things (Hebrews 1:2).

In our humanity, we are often impressed with the delivery system that God may choose to speak to us. In the Bible, we see God speaking in various and different ways. There are three occasions in the Bible where God spoke in an audible voice. God sent many prophets, both men and women, to speak to His people. God spoke through a donkey to Balaam. (Numbers 22:2830) God wrote upon the wall in the book of Daniel. (Daniel 5:5) God speaks in the hearts of His people and the writer to the Hebrews says (Hebrews 1:1), "God, who at various times and in various ways spoke in time past to the fathers by the prophets." Every time a prophet would speak to the people of Israel, he would usually begin his discourse with the phrase, "Thus says the Lord." Jesus never once said, "Thus says the Lord," because Jesus is the Lord. Instead of this, Jesus would say, "Verily, verily, I say unto you." (John 5:24) Jesus is God speaking to us. We are creatures of time and space. Imagine if I had met you 50 years ago and spoken to you. For us human beings, there is a good possibility that you may well have forgotten the words that I spoke 50 years ago; it is also quite possible that I may have forgotten those words. We forget, we get distracted, and we change over the course of time. It is vital that we realize that when God speaks, He is speaking to us now. If Jesus were to appear to you in a vision right now and speak to you, it would not be any more immediate or up to date than you opening the Bible and reading any verse within it. When God said to Moses, "I am the Lord who heals you" (Exodus 15:26), that is not simply a record of something God once said thousands of years ago. God is saying that right now to every person alive on planet Earth. God lives outside of time and space in eternity, and when He speaks, He speaks in the eternal now; every word from God is a word to you and me right now.

One of my favorite chapters in the entire Bible is the first chapter of 2nd Peter. In a real sense, this epistle is like Peter's last will and testament to the church. Peter begins the epistle by reminding the reader that he will soon leave planet earth. He will soon die just as Jesus showed him (Luke 21:36). In the first chapter of 2nd Peter, Peter, now a much older man, recounts the story of the Mount of Transfiguration, many years after the original event. For most of the contemporary readers of Peter, they were not alive when this took place. They had probably heard rumors of this, or been taught it through the various teachers in the first century church. In fact, Peter is writing to these Christians, proclaiming, "I was there; I stood on the mountain. I saw the glory of God. I heard with my own physical ears the audible voice of God speaking to his Son." (2 Peter 1:1718)

What an incredible claim. Peter then goes on to say something extraordinary. After recounting this incredible story,

Peter then admonishes the Christians. They have a more sure word from God than this experience. (2 Peter 1:19) Peter is saying that there is something more sure, more solid, more reliable than standing on a mountain and beholding the glory of Jesus. There is something more sure than having Moses and Elijah point to Jesus (the law and the prophets). There is something more certain than hearing the audible voice of God speak about Jesus. What is this more sure thing? Peter says that the very written Word of God is more sure than any vision, any manifestation, or any experience that we can ever have.

"Holy men of God spoke as they were moved by the Holy Spirit" (2 Peter 1:21).

As we continue to examine our foundational beliefs about God's Word, there is perhaps nothing more glorious than this: God is a God of integrity. God cannot lie; He is utterly and absolutely committed to everything He has said. God has never failed once in the entire universe to uphold His Word. This can seem like a foreign concept to us as human beings. Even with the most honest person we could ever meet, there is always some degree of a gap between what we do and what we say.

Many years ago in France, I had an open vision. I was taking a shower, praying in tongues as I am wont to do. Suddenly, my apartment disappeared, and I saw a vision of two hands moving together and then moving apart. These hands would nearly touch, and then they would move quite far away. I knew God was trying to communicate something to me, but I did not know what. In my heart, I said, "Lord, what are you trying to say to me?" The Holy Spirit answered me and said, "Integrity is measured by the distance between what we do, and what we say, between our words, and our actions." The Lord said to me, "With some people, it is like this," and I saw the two hands move quite far away. The Lord continued, "With other people, it is like this," and the hands moved quite closely together. Then the Lord said to me, "With me, it is this," and I saw the two hands come completely together. What God says is what God does. God is absolutely one with His Word.

"Not one word has failed of all the good things that the Lord your God promised concerning you. All have come to pass for you; not one of them has failed." Joshua 23:14

There is something glorious that occurs in our hearts when we realize that God's Word contains a promise, from somebody who cannot lie and cannot fail. All of the resources of heaven are backed behind God's Word. I grew up in the United Kingdom, and in the UK, we would utilize pound sterling for currency. All of my adult life while in the UK, I was accustomed to dealing with banknotes issued by the Bank of England. Until recently, all British banknotes contained an image of the Queen of England (Queen Elizabeth II), and each British banknote would contain the words: "I promise to pay the bearer on demand the sum of... 10 pounds." Simply put, the banknote was only a piece of paper, and yet it contained a promise, signed by the Secretary of the Treasury of the Queen, to guarantee that the bearer of this note could be reimbursed for the sum of 10 pounds. Basically, each British banknote is a signed promise from the Queen. We employ the same concept with a check. We fill in the amount on the check, the recipient to whom the check is addressed, and then we sign our name at the bottom of that check as a guarantee that they can take that paper to the bank and treat it like money. We live in a fallen world, to some degree at least. People will write checks that they cannot or will not honor. The Bible that you hold in your hands is God's written check to everybody who believes. It is signed in His name.

"God has exalted His word above all His name." Psalm 138:2

For many years, I would read this verse and simply thought it was a poetic expression. One day, I began to actually think through what the words say. Simply put, this verse is obvious. God's name is only as good as His Word. If God does not keep His Word, His name is empty of worth. If you write a check and sign your name on it, but you do not keep your word, your name will drop in value. The same thing is true with God's Word. When we realize these glorious truths, suddenly, faith becomes easy. We do not need to think about our faith; rather, we think about God's faithfulness to His Word. When we realize that God cannot fail His Word, it is easy to have confidence and walk upon that Word. People trusted in the Titanic when it was declared to be an unsinkable ship. Their faith was obviously misplaced in the word of the shipbuilders. But the God of the universe has declared that we can walk on His Word. He upholds all things by the power of His Word (Romans 4:21).

"Forever, oh Lord, your word is settled in heaven." (Psalm 119:89)

Every time God speaks, it is completely settled in the courts of heaven. God's word is the most concrete thing in the universe. It literally sustains everything in the universe. When we engage with God's word, we engage with a settled matter. The challenge for you and me as believers is to settle it in our hearts, the word that is already settled in heaven. It is one thing to affirm that God's word is absolutely true in heaven, but is it absolutely true in the heart of the believer? For us to live in accordance with what God has declared, the challenge for the believer is not to alter or persuade God. Our objective is not to convince God to uphold His word. Rather, our challenge is to establish God's word in our hearts. When the settled word in heaven becomes a settled word in our hearts, then we are truly in faith, and we are assured to see God's hand at work in our lives.

"Who has believed our report? And to whom is the arm of the Lord revealed?" (Isaiah 53:1)

This verse contains two questions. The answer to the first question is found in the answer to the second question. The arm of the Lord will always be revealed to the one who has believed (in his heart) God's report (God's written word). Have you ever experienced a failure of faith? I believe that most of us can relate to times and seasons in our lives when we thought we were believing God for something that did not come to pass. We often attempt various methods to come up with explanations to justify why we experience these failures. I believe the answer is simple for those who understand this truth. The problem does not lie in heaven; the problem lies within our own hearts. When the disciples inquired of Jesus why they experienced failure (Mark 9), Jesus did not mince his words. He immediately pointed to the root of the problem and said, "Because of your unbelief." Jesus described the failure of the disciples to set the boy free from demon oppression not due to any strange concept of God's but simply due to their incapacity to believe. I am sure that to those around them it sounded as if they knew what they were doing, but as Jesus pointed out, they doubted in their hearts whether the word they would speak would come to pass.

"And Jesus answered them, 'Have faith in God. Truly, I say to you, whoever says to this mountain, "Be taken up and thrown into the sea," and does not doubt in his heart, but believes that what he says will come to pass, it will be done for him. Therefore I tell you, whatever you ask in prayer, believe that you have received it, and it will be yours.'" (Mark 11:2224)

I encourage you, if you have experienced a faith failure, not to allow your failures to determine your beliefs about God and His power. Rather than hiding behind facile explanations and developing doctrine out of our failures, let us come back to the Bible and to Jesus with simple, childlike faith. Jesus encouraged the disciples in Mark chapter 9 after their faith failure to seek Him in prayer and fasting. He said, "This kind [of unbelief] can come out only by prayer and fasting." (Mark 9:29 NKJV) How then can we learn to settle God's word in our hearts? In a sense, this is not something we can do by willpower alone. It takes the work of the Holy Spirit to take the truth of God's word and write them upon the tablet of our hearts. Paul spoke about this. He compared under the old covenant God writing with His finger on tablets of stone. Paul says under the new covenant, God is now writing upon the tablets of our hearts. (2 Corinthians 3:3 NKJV) While we cannot simply choose to believe in our hearts as an act of our will, there are things we can do that will cause truth to penetrate our hearts. When we pay attention to God's word, truth begins to move from our heads to our hearts.

"My son, attend to my words, incline your ear to my sayings, keep them in the midst of your heart, keep them before your eyes for they [my words], are life to those who find them and health to all of your flesh." (Proverbs 4:2022 NKJV)

When we meditate upon the word of God, truth moves from our heads to our hearts. Renewing our mind means more than simply learning a Bible verse in a mechanical fashion. Whenever we think about something, our imagination begins to activate, and our heart begins to engage with that truth. Most of us have learned this in the negative rather than the positive of God's word. Everybody knows how to worry. Let me explain the process. We think about something (which may not even be true), as we think about this thing, our imagination begins to engage, and we begin to see all the ways this could affect our life. As we begin to think about these things, we begin to feel the corresponding emotions that are connected with this, which in turn causes us to begin the cycle and think about these things again. God designed us with the capacity to engage with thoughts in this way. If we will learn to meditate upon God's word, our hearts will engage with that truth sooner or later.

Another powerful way that we can bring truth from our minds into our hearts is simply by speaking God's word out loud with our mouths. There is a simple Bible principle that is reflexive, that is to say, it works both ways: Whatever is in your heart in abundance will come out of your mouth. Whatever you put in your mouth in abundance will sink into your heart.

Out of the abundance of the heart, the mouth speaks (Matthew 12:34 NKJV).

If we will take the word of God, even if we are not entirely sure that we believe it, and speak it, we will begin to believe it. The epistle of James says that our tongue is like the rudder of a ship. It can set a course, and over time, it will move that large ship in that direction. You set a course over your own life by the words that you speak. If you will begin to proclaim God's word every day in abundance, after a season, that word will settle in your heart. I remember as a young minister many years ago struggling to trust God for finances to meet the needs of my family and ministry. There was a season in which the Lord challenged me to spend 30 minutes a day proclaiming verses such as, "My God shall supply all of my needs according to His riches in glory by Christ Jesus." (Philippians 4:19 NKJV) I remember after a few days doing this, in my heart, there was a cry, "God, I simply do not believe this." I heard the still small voice of the Holy Spirit say, "I am not asking you to feel something but to act upon my word." Over time, that word was settled in my heart, and I have discovered that God's word settled in heaven, and also settled in my heart, has settled every financial need I have ever had in my life. I believe it is absolutely vital and imperative that we think through and develop a vision for this part of our spiritual life. If we do not take the time to do this, then by default, we are living without a vision in this area, and we will simply live an accidental Christian life. This is where the average Christian lives. As a pastor, I am only too aware of how few people never open the Bible from one week to another. For many people, it is only at the moment I will ask them to turn to a specific scripture that the Bible has been touched in the last week. I do not say that to condemn or belittle anybody, but it is vital that if we wish to live a flourishing Christian life, we develop an effective relationship with the Word of God. If I were to ask the average Christian how much time they have spent with God's word in the last 24 hours, most Christians would simply explain that the past day has been a busy one. That they do not know where all the time went, but they would reassure me (with a sincere heart) that they intend seriously to spend time with God's word tomorrow. The sad truth, of course, is that tomorrow never arrives. Today is the day of salvation, and today is the only day by which we can measure our lives and our walk with God.

What then would be an effective, and indeed, realistic vision for our own personal relationship with the Word of God? I would suggest that every believer should engage with the Word of God in the following ways:

We must begin by establishing some of the basic truths about what God's Word is, about God's integrity, and absolute commitment to His Word deep within our hearts. In the truth that we have already covered in this chapter (Psalm 119:89 NKJV).

On an ongoing basis, we should learn to practically engage with the Word of God in the following ways:

Reading God's Word. I would encourage everybody to have a plan or strategy to read through the Bible. Personally, I do not use a plan for reading through the Bible in one year. I believe that there are some parts of God's Word that we should major on, and others, which though they are important, are not of primary importance to the believer. Here is my own Bible reading plan. I set this down here not as an example of a perfect plan, but rather one that has served me well for many years, and I encourage you to adapt and change this to your own lifestyle and needs.

I divide the Bible into five different sections, and each day I try to read through between two and four chapters from each of the sections. If my time is short, I start at the top of this list and prioritize these parts first:

1. The Gospels and Book of Acts.
2. The New Testament Epistles.
3. The wisdom/poetry books Psalms, Proverbs, Ecclesiastes).
4. Old Testament history books.
5. Old Testament prophets.

I cycle through these five sections of the Bible. When I have finished reading through the books containing one of the sections, I simply turn back and begin again. In doing so, I will read through the entire Bible at least once a year, but I will also read through the Gospels, Epistles, and Wisdom books several times each year.

Secondly, I confess God's Word. To be clear, I define confession as speaking aloud the truth of God's Word (usually in the first person). I keep a looseleaf folder that I use for Bible verses that speak to me, that define my identity in Christ, and God's promises towards me. I've had this for many years, and in some measure each day I will add new verses to this book. I divide this book into subjects and sections that speak to my heart. When I confess or declare these verses, I am not simply going through the act of speaking them aloud, but rather, I am bringing them into my relationship with Father God. I am thanking Him that these things are true in my life, even if I do not currently see or feel them in this season.

Thirdly, I engage in the discipline of memorizing Bible verses. As I confess Bible verses out loud, I will also at the end of the verse declare the Bible reference that goes with that verse. A wonderful way of learning Bible verses by heart is to put them into your mouth and speak them out (including the reference). In doing so, in the same manner that we may learn a song, you will find that that Bible verse just rolls off your tongue, including the reference. This is a really useful skill for life, sharing your faith, and indeed, for teaching or other aspects of ministry.

Lastly, I would encourage every believer to engage in the process of studying God's Word. When we study, we approach God's Word through the lens of studying a particular theme, truth, or section of the Bible. In my own practice, I tend to take between one to three months to study a particular theme. When I do that, I will make a list of all the Bible verses or references that refer to that subject. I will also read Christian books on that subject. In coming before the Lord in prayer, I will take the time to allow Him to unfold that subject. One of the things that will really help me in this regard is to come and assemble a list of my questions concerning this subject. Rather than looking for answers (answers are easy), I will come and ask the Lord for questions that I can meditate upon. When I am studying a subject, my goal is to catch the heart of God and also grasp a high level, 50,000foot perspective on what God's Word is communicating about the subject. I always try to end these seasons of studying with practical applications.

Take some time to engage with these questions and write down a vision statement for how you wish to live out the rest of your life in relationship to the word of God.

Questions for Meditation

- *Are there ideas and scripts about this area of your life that heaven wants to rewrite in this season?*
- *What are the challenges you have in relation to this subject? Describe them as past, defeated, and nailed to the cross.*
- *What is the Lord displacing in your life? What new thing does He want to replace the old with?*
- *How does God define my identity?*
- *Describe the relationship that God is calling you to have with Him in this area.*
- *If God were saying "Yes and Amen", what would your request be?*
- *What would living in complete freedom, joy, and victory look like?*
- *What promise is God speaking over you in this season? What are the promises He is calling you to declare back to Him?*
- *What would transformation look like under your present circumstances?*
- *What would it take for you to develop a mindset, a lifestyle, a persona of fullness as a way of life?*
- *How are you called to minister to others?*

Chapter Five

The Life of Faith

"He who is born of God overcomes the world, and this is the victory that has overcome the world — our faith." (1 John 5:4)

God is a God of faith. Everything that God does operates and works by faith. Without faith, we cannot please God (Hebrews 11:6) and outside of faith, we can never access all that God has for us. If we desire to walk with God, we can never overlook the subject of faith. There are many wonderful aspects to the Christian life and journey with God, many wonderful subjects we can explore, but it is vital that we do not simply regard faith as merely one among many. Faith is simply the key that activates all the promises of God on our behalf.

"Without faith, it is impossible to please God." (Hebrews 11:6)
"Whatever is not from faith is sin." (Romans 14:23)
"All things are possible for one who believes." (Mark 9:23)
"For everyone who has been born of God overcomes the world. And this is the victory that has overcome the world—our faith." (1 John 5:4)

* * *

For many believers, faith can seem like an unattainable force that only super saints or special people seem to attain. I remember as a young believer reading about the lives of many great saints of the past. People like Smith Wigglesworth, who walked in an incredible place with God. I realized that at a young age, if I could figure out how to obtain faith, I could live in all the promises of God. I would "try to believe", and yet, it seemed that the more attempts I made to have faith, the more I struggled. Like many people, I experienced moments when I would pray for something and be certain, or at least, truly hopeful that God was going to answer, only to find myself disappointed. Like so many others, I lived with an intellectual belief that God would answer prayer, and yet the reality of unanswered prayer exerted an influence on my life and caused a lingering sensation that this stuff doesn't really work.

I began traveling as an evangelist in my late teens. As this ministry began to develop, I found myself in need of a good, reliable vehicle for ministry. At the time, I read the biography of a wonderful man of God called Colin Urquhart. In this book, Pastor Urquhart found himself in need of a ministry vehicle. He recounted how he had ordered a new car from a dealership by faith, without possessing the money for the purchase. Over the course of the next few days, money came in from all over the world, and he had paid for his car debt-free. After reading this book, I decided that if this worked for this well-known minister, it would also work for me. Together with a friend, I visited a local car dealership and ordered a good used car "by faith." Over the next few days, I waited for money to come in from all over the world. Of course, no money came, and after several days, I was obliged to visit the dealership and explain, much to the consternation of the dealer, that I did not possess the money to buy the car.

A few weeks later, I was attending a conference in the south of England. During one of the breaks, a lady approached me and inquired if I was believing in God for a car. I promptly responded affirmatively. The lady then conveyed her intention to donate her car to my ministry. She requested that I pray about it and mentioned that if I was interested, I should meet her in the parking lot at 12 noon. Gesturing through the window, she pointed out, "My car is that blue car right there." Subsequently, the lady returned to the meeting, while I, as you can imagine, headed to the parking lot to inspect the blue car. The only vehicle I could discern in the parking lot was a brand new, gleaming Jaguar, a luxurious British car with beautiful leather seats and walnut trim. I rejoined the meeting, but truthfully, all I could contemplate was myself traveling in this exquisite, luxurious car. At lunchtime, I encountered the lady again, who inquired if I was still interested in receiving the car. She escorted me to the parking lot directly to the Jaguar, and then past the Jaguar to an old, rusted blue car that was at least 25 years old. The car was in a dilapidated state. I suspect there had been chickens living in the back of the car. It took numerous attempts to even start the engine. When the car eventually spluttered to life, she handed me the keys and proudly stated, "There is your new car." Have you ever been angered with God? I was furious. I recall entering the restroom of the hotel, brandishing the keys towards heaven, and exclaiming to the Lord, "What do you call this?" Immediately, the Holy Spirit responded to my heart with a phrase I will never forget. He said to me, "That is the current measure of your faith. Instead of asking me to do greater things around you, ask me instead to enlarge the place of your faith in the inner man." I instantly grasped the message the Holy Spirit intended to convey, and it has been a principle by which I have lived and walked throughout all the days of my life. Since that moment, I have received many cars by faith. Much better, and indeed more expensive ones. And yes, I have learned the lesson, but I cannot simply emulate the faith of somebody else. I can be inspired by that faith, but I need to cultivate my own faith from my personal relationship with God and His word.

Let us take a few moments and go back to the basic principles of Faith.

- What is faith?
- How does Faith come?
- How do we grow in faith?

THE WORD

Simply put, faith is confidence in God. When God promises that He will do something, faith simply takes God at His word and believes that He will fulfill it. When God declares He has already accomplished something, faith simply trusts His declaration. When God assures that if we ask anything in His name, He will do it, faith praises and believes the answer is accomplished the moment we pray, not when visible results are seen. It is a wonderful lesson to learn, but the problems are never on God's end of the equation. Faith has very little to do with ourselves. We do not need to examine our own ability to believe; faith depends entirely upon God's word and what He says in His word.

"In the beginning was the Word, and the Word was with God, and the Word was God." (John 1:1)

* * *

For most of us, our words do not perfectly represent who we are. We may say one thing but do another. When God speaks, He is 100% committed to what He says. We know God perfectly by His word, and we can utterly rely upon it.

"Heaven and earth will pass away, but My words will never pass away." (Matthew 24:35)

I realized this truth at a rather young age, as a new Christian. I was part of a church in the UK that believed God could heal the sick, yet if we were honest, it hardly ever seemed to happen in our experience. We became adept at devising clever explanations to justify why a person was not healed. I often quipped that people began to go bald in my church because they had hands laid on them so many times. Many began to question God and inquire why healing seemed to hardly ever occur, despite faithful Christians praying. As a teenager, I decided that I did not want to preach something that was not true. I set my heart to fast and pray and find an answer. After seeking God for several days, He gave me an answer that revolutionized my life. He showed me that the answer I was seeking was simply the Bible, the word of God. I realized that although we professed love for the Bible and honored it, we did not accord it the same reverence as we would if Jesus were physically present with us. We deemed God's word important, but not as important as Jesus Himself. Nobody would have ever articulated those words, but we can discern what we believe by our actions, not solely by the statement of faith on our website. I realized that if Jesus were to walk into my church on a Sunday morning, radiating all of His glory, and then proclaimed that He had come to heal the sick, there would not be one person who doubted that they would be instantly healed. Nobody would doubt Jesus if He were present in person. I understood that when we have His word, Jesus is present. Jesus in person would have no more power than His word in His absence.

"Where the word of a king is, there is power" (Ecclesiastes 8:4).

"Heaven and earth will pass away, but My words will by no means pass away." Matthew 24:35 (NKJV)

If we wish to grow in faith, then we need to spend time with the word of God. We need to learn to trust the word. We need to come to a place where God's word is more real than the world around us. We need to take God at His word. Simply put, to trust God, is to trust His word.

The second key to understanding faith is to recognize that faith is not merely an intellectual endeavor. We can comprehend doctrine and teaching with our minds, but faith is of the heart. We cannot simply choose to believe as an act of our will. However, what we can do as a matter of our will is choose to engage our eyes, ears, mind, and mouth with God's word, and by doing so, our hearts will begin to follow. In English, we say "to learn by heart." Interestingly, in Jewish culture, this would be phrased "as to learn by mouth."

"Out of the abundance of the heart, the mouth speaks." (Matthew 12:34)

Faith is not the result of striving; faith is the result of resting. You know when you are in faith because trusting God becomes natural and normal without any effort. We establish faith in our heart in two ways:

Firstly, by spending time with the word and allowing it to enter into our hearts.

Secondly, by acting upon the word of God and proving the word of God in our own personal experience. The more we develop the personal history of acting upon the word of God, the more we will build up a natural, normal, and unconscious faith that God means what he says and says what he means. At this stage, faith becomes easy to us.

Hebrews 11:1, Amplified Bible

"Now faith is the assurance (title deed, confirmation) of things hoped for (divinely guaranteed), and the evidence of things not seen [the conviction of their reality—faith comprehends as fact what cannot be experienced by the physical senses]."

The third step to understanding faith is so simple, yet it is one that is usually overlooked by most Christians. Faith will accept that something is done, accomplished, and completed even without the evidence of the five physical senses (touch, taste, smell, hearing, and sight). Faith believes that something is accomplished without seeing any physical evidence to corroborate that fact. This is not denial or positive thinking. Faith accepts as a real fact the result of God's word being accepted.

The clearest example of faith is seen in the story of Jesus and the fig tree in Mark 11. In this passage, Jesus notices a fig tree and goes to see if it has any fruit. When he discovers that it does not, Jesus curses the fig tree. Notice that all Jesus says is the end result that he wishes to happen: "Let no one eat fruit from you ever again." The disciples who are with Jesus hear him say this but do not see any visible change in the tree. The next day when passing the same spot, the disciples notice the tree is completely dead, dried up from the roots. Jesus then explains to the disciples the principles of faith by which he lives and by which they can also live.

Mark 11:24
"Therefore, I say to you, whatever things you ask when you pray, believe that you receive them, and you will have them."

The key is to believe that you have received when you pray, not when you see something happen. If we can grasp and implement this principle, our whole lives will be changed, and we will become men and women of faith. It is not faith when we believe that something may happen at some future date. Faith takes God at His word and believes that the thing is done based on the word, and the word alone.

The final key to understanding the life of faith is that faith revolves around action. There exists a fallacy that the goal of faith is to establish internal beliefs within the heart. If our faith in God only leads us to a point where we possess correct beliefs but they fail to alter how we live, then that is not genuine faith. This is merely mental ascent or intellectual faith. You can discern a person's beliefs by observing their actions.

There is a reflexive law at play here that nobody can evade: whatever we believe in our heart will manifest as actions in our life. However, it is equally true that whatever we act upon in our life can influence and shape the beliefs in our heart. John G. Lake, one of the great missionary heroes of faith, once said, "I can act my way into believing much quicker than I can believe my way into acting." While that might not be entirely theologically accurate, I believe I concur with the essence and sentiment of what Lake is trying to express.

Faith necessitates action, and that very action will internally strengthen and deepen our faith. I once conducted a comprehensive study of every healing miracle recounted in the four Gospels, both individual accounts and corporate instances of healing. My objective was to examine each biblical narrative to discern the context, Jesus' actions and words, and what the recipients of his healing power both did and said. If you ever wish to engage in an enlightening Bible study, I highly recommend this approach to you. In nearly every instance of healing, Jesus would instruct the person to act upon his word.

Stretch out your withered hand (Mark 3:5 NKJV).

Go show yourself to the priest (Luke 5:14 NKJV).

Arise, and walk (John 5:8 NKJV).

You can measure your faith by measuring your willingness to act upon God's word.

The other key I found in relation to Jesus's healing ministry was speaking God's word. There are times when it may be hard to find a physical action that we can engage in. There are healing situations where we cannot arise and walk, or stretch out our withered hand. But there is no situation we will ever be in, we cannot choose to speak the word of God. Learning the power of proclaiming God's word in spite of every circumstance and contradicting sensory evidence is a powerful manifestation of faith. If we claim to have faith, but we do not have action with our faith, then we are in error. James says faith without corresponding actions is dead (James 2:17).

VISION OF A LIFE OF FAITH

So what would it look like to live a life of faith? The perfect answer to this question is simply to look at the life of Jesus. To live a life of faith is to live from above. To live a life of faith is to live not by bread alone, but by every word that proceeds from the mouth of God. The Bible says four times that the just will live by faith (Habakkuk 2:4, Romans 1:17, Galatians 3:11, Hebrews 10:38).

To live by faith means to have faith involved in every part of one's life. There should be no part of our life which does not come under the influence of our faith. Living by faith would mean that we believe in God for:

The keeping power of God in our life: Psalm 121:78
The Lord's healing and health: Exodus 15:26
The guidance and leading of the Holy Spirit: John 16:13
Our satisfaction: Psalm 107:9
Our joy: Psalm 16:11
Overcoming sin: Romans 6:14
The one who answers our prayers: 1 John 5:1415
Our source of life and fellowship: 1 John 1:3

* * *

We need to practice bringing faith into every element of our lives. If we only ever attempt to use our faith in crisis situations, then we will find it often fails us when we need it most. Instead, if we endeavor to bring faith into every small and large part of our lives, no area should be exempt from the glorious walk of faith in God's promises.

Begin the life of faith today. Take the time to sit down and envision yourself as a man or woman of faith.

Questions for Meditation

- *Are there ideas and scripts about this area of your life that heaven wants to rewrite in this season?*

- *What are the challenges you have in relation to this subject? Describe them as past, defeated, and nailed to the cross.*

- *What is the Lord displacing in your life? What new thing does He want to replace the old with?*

- *How does God define my identity?*

- *Describe the relationship that God is calling you to have with Him in this area.*

- *If God were saying "Yes and Amen", what would your request be?*

- *What would living in complete freedom, joy, and victory look like?*

- *What promise is God speaking over you in this season? What are the promises He is calling you to declare back to Him?*

- *What would transformation look like under your present circumstances?*

- *What would it take for you to develop a mindset, a lifestyle, a persona of fullness as a way of life?*

- *How are you called to minister to others?*

Chapter Six

Understanding Our Soul

May the God of peace sanctify you, holy spirit, soul, body. (1 Thessalonians 5:23)

Possessing your soul in patience. (Luke 21:19)

In this chapter, we will explore what it means to have a vision for our soul. We will answer questions about what our soul is, what God requires of our soul, and what it would mean for us to flourish in this life, and the next, as God intended our soul to fully live.

It is common for people to use the terms spirit and soul interchangeably, sometimes assuming they are the same. God loves us even if we have bad theology, but bad theology can cause us to step out of God's life. It is important that we understand our makeup as spirit, soul, and body, and that we allow God to work in each of these areas of our lives. It is possible to be a born-again believer, to love God, and yet not allow your soul to change in any way. Much of the pain and misery believers go through in life is not the result of others or

Satan; some of our problems come from our own soul. In this chapter, we will explore how to allow the freedom that is ours in Christ to permeate every realm of your mind, your will, and your emotions – your soul.

What is a soul? Simply put, our soul is our mind, will, and emotions.

MIND

There is a difference between the mind and the brain. The brain is the physical organ seen and perceived by science; it can be damaged, operated upon, and manipulated. The mind is our ability to think and understand. We could compare our brain to a computer, and our mind to the software that runs upon it.

EMOTIONS

Our emotions are our abilities to feel, to enjoy (and indeed to suffer sometimes). They are the internal parts of our being that experience joy, sadness, anger, fear, surprise, disgust, love, hate,, grief, anxiety, excitement, guilt, shame, jealousy, loneliness, gratitude, hope, etc.

WILL

Our will, or volition, is the part of us that chooses and makes decisions for our lives. While it can be helpful for illustrative purposes to separate the soul into those three parts, it is important to realize how much these three areas are interlocked and interwoven with each other. People often talk about having free will, but our will is often in bondage to our emotions and our mind. When the mind begins to think upon something, our emotions usually engage, turning small thoughts into powerful emotions.

Each of these areas of our soul functions at both a conscious and unconscious level. With our will, we can make a choice to do something. I could decide right now to raise my arm and then to lower it. Try this right now, and yet, while my will was exerting a conscious choice upon my body, my will was also unconsciously making thousands of other choices. My will was operating all of the internal systems of my body at an unconscious level. I would only be aware of these internal choices when something is wrong or goes amiss. The same is true for our thoughts and our emotions. We may consciously think of something. In my mind, I can count from one to ten right now, and yet we are also constantly thinking of things, running scripts within our minds, that we are not aware of. So often, these internal dialogues, these scripts running on the inside of us, will dictate the choices of our will. The same is true for our emotions and yet at a more subtle level from our experience. There are times we are very aware of our emotions, and yet other times when we are experiencing something emotionally that we are not consciously aware of.

In the Garden of Eden, God said to Adam, "In the day you eat of the tree, you will surely die." (Genesis 2:17) Adam did not die physically that day, nor did he die spiritually. He still had the ability to think, to choose, to experience emotions; the part that died was the spiritual component. Outside of Jesus, we are spiritually dead. When we are born again, our body and soul are not born again. Rather, our spirit is reborn in Jesus. As a believer, you have a brand new spirit, one that is united with Jesus. (1 Corinthians 6:17). It is important to realize that our soul is not transformed when we are born again. Our spirit has been made new. When Jesus returns, we will receive a new glorified body, but in this life, our soul remains the same. God's plan is that the spirit enters into and transforms the life of our soul here on Earth. It is empowering to realize that, even though we are God's children, we still have the same flesh and memories that we have had all our lives. We still carry the same emotional baggage throughout our lives. We become citizens of a new nation in a moment, but we need to actively embrace the process of learning to speak the language of that nation, to think thoughts and scripts of heaven. In this chapter, we will explore this process and how we can have an effective vision of our soul prospering in this life.

"Therefore, I urge you, brothers and sisters, in view of God's mercy, to offer your bodies as a living sacrifice, holy and pleasing to God—this is your true and proper worship. Do not conform to the pattern of this world, but be transformed by the renewing of your mind. Then you will be able to test and approve what God's will is—his good, pleasing and perfect will." Romans 12:12

We have stated in a previous chapter, and indeed, the Bible clearly states that our old man is absolutely dead. Why, then, does it seem as though this old man is very much alive in the experience of the average person? Is, as Mark Twain once quipped, "the rumors of his death are greatly exaggerated"? How do we resolve this anomaly? More to the point, how do we apply the truth of the Bible in a way that will cause us to live in victory?

The old man is indeed dead. (Romans 6:6 NKJV). So do the dead live? Well, in a certain sense, yes. The old man lives within the memories, choices, and emotions of our soul. To return to our technology analogy, we have a brand new operating system, downloaded from the cloud, yet we are still filled with the bugs, viruses, and damaged software of our old hard drive. Our soul (mind, will, and emotions) has been mentored by every single experience we have walked through. We still bear the scars of the fall from God. We were created by God and created for glorious fellowship with God. Because of sin, we have been separated from God. There is a deep longing and yearning in the depths of our soul for acceptance and fellowship. So often, this is manifested in our lives as rejection. Outside of Christ, our primary identity is out of an orphan, longing for acceptance and love. We may mask and hide this in a thousand different ways, and yet it is impossible to separate ourselves from the gravitational pull of this longing upon our souls.

Our fallen nature has molded our soul with desires outside of God. This old nature has been dealt with at the cross of Calvary, and yet in spite of this, we still live with the habits, memories, choices, and scripts that we have developed over a long period of time. In both a conscious and unconscious manner. The immediate world in which we live also exerts a massive influence upon our soul, in ways that we are not always aware of. The information we constantly assimilate, the people with whom we frequent, the very culture in which we are bathed, will shape and mentor our soul into the person we are. This is often in opposition to God. The apostle Paul warns us in Romans 12:12 not to be squeezed or molded into the shape of this world but rather to allow the word of God to change us into his image and likeness.

We are all influenced by the culture in which we live.

Cultures can exert sway upon us in ways we do not always recognize. Culture functions as the collective memories, assumptions, values, and perceived understanding that we have inherited over a long period of time from previous generations. I am influenced and changed in my personality today by the culture in which I have been brought up. Many of the inflection points of this culture were defined hundreds of years ago. We have received and inherited a lens through which we look upon the world, passed on to us from our forefathers.

There are nation states that have endured many years of suffering through preceding generations. For example, the Russian people have suffered greatly for centuries under the czars, communist dictatorship, and postSoviet leaders. The choices of our will, the thoughts, and internal dialogues of our minds, and the emotions we experience, can often be the result of inherited patterns we have received from multiple generations. The United States, for example, is a very positive culture. America still carries the DNA of pioneers. By and large, most of the current population of America came to that nation as immigrants, with a desire to take risks and build a better life. The same principle can be applied to the descendants of those who were brought to America as slaves. We can change the laws of a nation and create perfect equality by federal decree, and yet our souls still carry the collective choices, emotions, and thought patterns that we have inherited from preceding generations.

Another area that often impacts the soul is the domain of trauma. We have all walked through experiences in our own personal lives that have shaped and formed us, molding our soul into the person that we currently are. When we experience something traumatic, it has the tendency to imprint that experience upon our soul. These traumatic experiences will then indelibly inscribe conscious and unconscious choices, patterns, and emotions upon us that become very hard to change or erase. All of us go through experiences of trauma at different levels.

As a teenager, I was involved in a serious car wreck. I was in the passenger seat of a car when the driver lost control at around 90 miles an hour. The car spun around and flipped over several times, at which point I lost consciousness. I regained consciousness in an ambulance on the way to a hospital. I emerged from the accident with merely a few cuts and bruises, and walked for several days with a cane. There were no longterm physical effects from this traumatic experience. My soul, however, was deeply impacted by this accident. For many years following this incident, I found it nearly impossible to be a passenger in a vehicle. I had no issue personally driving a vehicle, but whenever I was in the role of a passenger, fear and terror would grip my inner being in a way that I find hard to describe. This was not rational fear. There were many instances where I was seized with terror in the passenger seat of a car, even if the driver was only traveling at 30 miles an hour. On a rational level, I knew that even if the car were to crash, there would not be a significant amount of damage at 30 miles an hour. But fear is not governed by reason. We cannot simply eradicate fear with a conscious, rational decision.

The good news is that we have a glorious Savior in Christ Jesus, the Lord. God has already completely saved our spirit. At a future stage, God will save and glorify our physical bodies. Right now in this life, we can experience the glorious, saving power of the Lord Jesus Christ in our soul. Jesus said, "You will know the truth and the truth will set you free" (John 8:32). "He whom the Son sets free is free indeed" (John 8:36). Let us explore and discover how we step into freedom in the soulful realm and define a vision of us, living as free men and women to the glory of God. How does transformation work in our soul?

The first key to the transformation of our soul is always that of repentance. It is important that we do not confuse biblical repentance with religious ideas of penance and penitence. Repentance is all about realignment. Repentance is about coming back to God, in the same way we initially came to Him. Repentance involves our coming to God and acknowledging anything and everything that is wrong in our lives. The base level truth of all biblical transformation is that change and transformation come to us exclusively through the power of the cross. Human psychology and psychoanalysis can help us uncover and diagnose some of the problems in our soul, but it lacks any ability to wash and cleanse us from sin. We need to grasp the truth that all the problems in our soul find their roots in the fall of man. Every single problem we have in the soulful realm comes directly or indirectly from this source.

It is important to note that not every problem we have in the realm of the soul comes directly from that person's individual sin, but rather from the fall of mankind into sin. We cannot psychoanalyze sin. We cannot self help our way out of sin. We cannot medicate our way out of sin. We cannot rationalize or ignore the reality of sin in our life.

"What can wash away our sins? Nothing but the blood of Jesus."

It is vital for the Christian that we learn to repent in a biblical way. As a pastor, I have encountered many people who struggle with repentance. By definition, when one is in sin, one usually begins to feel shame and the desire to hide from God. In that state, Satan will come as the accuser of the brethren, telling us that God is disgusted with us and will not accept us. It cannot be overstressed. The key to repentance is understanding that God wishes us to be in right relation with Him more than we do.

How should we then repent?

1. We come to God and acknowledge our sin before him.
2. We ask him to forgive and cleanse us of sin.
3. We believe by faith in his word alone, without any emotion or sensation, that our sins are now completely forgiven.
4. We rejoice and thank God and proclaim that we are clean before him based on his promise and his promise alone.

The key to walking out this new life in the arena of our soul is to practice the discipline of starting with our will, thoughts, and allowing our emotions to follow. At first, this can seem counterintuitive and something which we find difficult to implement. The vast majority of believers have many years of practicing allowing their emotions to dominate their life and willpower. Our emotions have an uncanny way of pretending to be ourselves

. When we feel something, we instinctively believe that it is true, because it is a current dominant experience. Learning that you can experience something, but the thing you are experiencing may not even be real is a powerful lesson in life. Just for the purposes of illustration, imagine if a person came to you today and told you that somebody close to you had just been involved in a terrible fatal accident. You would immediately begin to feel sorrow, grief, shock, etc, in the realm of your emotions. If you then subsequently found out that that person had lied to you, all of those negative emotions would immediately disappear. It is vital that we realize that Satan is a liar. He is a master at enabling us to believe things that, from God's vantage point, are not true. At the foundational level, all sin is based on emotion. James chapter 1, verse 1415 says:

"But each one is tempted when he is drawn away by his own desires and enticed. Then, when desire has conceived, it gives birth to sin; and sin, when it is full grown, brings forth death." The way to live in this new transformed life is to engage in the daily practice and discipline of submitting our will to God. We need to practice as a conscious choice of our will to think on whatever God is saying in his word.

"Finally, brethren, whatever things are true, whatever things are noble, whatever things are just, whatever things are pure, whatever things are lovely, whatever things are of good report, if there is any virtue and if there is anything praiseworthy— meditate on these things" (Philippians 4:8).

When our will and focus in life are anchored on the things of God, I can absolutely guarantee you that we will begin to feel emotions in line with God's plan for our lives. We need to establish a clear vision of how to practice this in normal life, and so embed this in the fabric of our souls that it becomes the way that we normally function. We need to learn to practice the way of the kingdom of God. The most powerful way I know to affect permanent transformation in your soul is the practice of confessing or declaring God's word over your life. By definition, when we take God's word and speak it out over our own lives, we are engaging our will with the things of God, we are thinking about the word of God, and we are actually putting our own mouth and ears into the practice of speaking and hearing the word of God. I encourage you to develop your own personal daily discipline of speaking and proclaiming God's word over your life. Become the prophet of your own life.

The second key to walking out God's transformation in the area of our soul is to realize that in the kingdom of God, things function in the opposite way of the world. Our pattern outside of God works in this way:

1. We commence with our emotions: "How do I feel about this?"
2. We engage our mind with what we are feeling in our emotions.
3. We allow our will to be dictated by our emotions and our thoughts about them.

In this manner, we subjugate our will to our experiential emotions and our thoughts. In the kingdom of God, God plans and purposes that we function in the opposite manner.

1. We commence with our will. We choose to fix our will on whatever God would desire. "Not my will but yours be done" (Luke 22:42).
2. We renew our mind with the word of God; we contemplate what God says in his word (Colossians 3:1).
3. We allow our emotions to assist us and propel us in the direction of our thoughts, which are in line with God's will.

* * *

96

When we learn to live this way, our powerful emotions are actually propelling us like wind in a sailing ship into the plans and purposes of God, not away from them as before. When we learn to function in this way we allow the life of our soul to be determined by the life of the Spirit.

Questions for Meditation

- *Are there ideas and scripts about this area of your life that heaven wants to rewrite in this season?*

- *What are the challenges you have in relation to this subject? Describe them as past, defeated, and nailed to the cross.*

- *What is the Lord displacing in your life? What new thing does He want to replace the old with?*

- *How does God define my identity?*

- *Describe the relationship that God is calling you to have with Him in this area.*

- *If God were saying "Yes and Amen", what would your request be?*

- *What would living in complete freedom, joy, and victory look like?*

- *What promise is God speaking over you in this season? What are the promises He is calling you to declare back to Him?*

- *What would transformation look like under your present circumstances?*

- *What would it take for you to develop a mindset, a lifestyle, a persona of fullness as a way of life?*

- *How are you called to minister to others?*

Chapter Seven

The Life of Worship

We become like the thing that we worship. We were made to worship; we cannot help but worship; the only question is, what will we worship?

Worship is one of the most glorious experiences a person can ever embark upon. There are many things with which we can fill our Christian lives. We have many calls, many legitimate activities. There are many things we need to learn and engage in, but there is nothing in the world more important than worship. Throughout all eternity, we will be worshiping God. In this chapter, I invite you to embark on a journey of worship. I invite you to learn and grow. I believe if we are going to become the worshiping community and the people that God is looking for upon the Earth, then we need to be willing to leave behind many of our religious ideas and connotations concerning worship.

I believe that Jesus is returning for a glorious bride. (Revelation 19:7) I believe that Jesus is not returning for a church that looks like the early church. I believe that Jesus is returning for a church that looks exactly like him.

* * *

When Adam saw Eve for the first time, his reaction was, "bone of my bone, flesh of my flesh." (Genesis 2:23) In effect, Adam was saying, "This bride is the perfect counterpart for me. I am ultimately happy, pleased, and satisfied with God's choice of a bride for me." I believe that is exactly what Jesus will say when he returns for his bride. We have sometimes adopted the conception that Jesus is returning to transform his bride. When our hopes for transformation rest in the second coming of Christ rather than in the finished works of Christ we are stepping into error. Transformation was signed, sealed, and delivered on the cross at Calvary. When Jesus returns, that is a full consummation of that experience.

I believe that in the days to come before the return of Jesus, worship will be the thing that transforms us more than any other. More than any teaching, more than any program, more than any self-help or efforts of our own transformation. Our transformation will come by beholding and becoming.

"We are beholding as in a mirror the glory of the Lord, and are being changed into the same image" (2 Corinthians 3:18, NKJV).

When we worship, we encounter God.
When we worship, we step out of this world and into the next.
When we worship, we bring the presence of heaven down upon the Earth and change the atmosphere. (Psalm 22:3)

Our highest call, our greatest purpose, and our primary identity are found in that of worship. Throughout all eternity, our chief occupation will be worship, and the experience of God. (Revelation 22:3) If that is a true statement, then I believe we should embrace that occupation and identity here and now in this life.

What do you think about when you hear the word worship? What are your associations and memories with worship? Probably, for most of us, our understanding of worship comes from the different church experiences that we have lived and walked through in our own Christian life. This could range from more traditional church worship, with liturgy and hymns, and ranging to a more contemporary pop/rock style of worship. I think there is both legitimacy and value in all of these expressions of worship. Having traveled for many years in ministry and visited thousands of churches in over 30 nations, I have come to the conclusion that all styles of worship are equally valid, but more importantly, that the challenge that lies before us, and the body of Christ has very little to do with style, presentation, or even excellence in terms of musicianship.

I believe that worship is a revelation. Without a revelation that can only come from the Holy Spirit regarding worship, I believe we are locked into human that may have some minimalistic value but completely miss the heart of God.

For the first few years of my Christian life, I was part of a spiritual Church in the UK where worship services were similar to most of the churches of that time (or equally of today). We would sing songs about God, we would celebrate, we would sing songs of worship, we would raise our hands in adoration. If you were to really drill down to its basic, foundational truths, worship for me, at that time, came down to singing songs about God. I think we had an understanding of giving God glory, and that praise was due to him. But to a large degree, this was very much what I would term a horizontal experience. That is to say, there would be a group of people in a room singing songs which would reaffirm to our collective group Christian truths. Is there anything wrong with this? Absolutely not. I believe that this is an important and valid part of worship. In the late 1990s, I had an experience with Jesus which changed and transformed my life, but equally my understanding and perception of worship.

Without going into the details of that encounter, Jesus appeared to me and declared to me that he loved me. I have never met a single Christian who does not agree that Jesus loves them. What became a revelation to me in that moment was the kind, or quality of love, that Jesus felt towards me. Without ever reducing it to words, I had always lived with a basic understanding that we have a loving and benevolent God, who in his kindness and fatherly love, has mercy, compassion, and regard towards his children. What I came to realize in this experience was that Jesus loved his bride, of whom I was part, with a fiery, passionate, and romantic love that could never be quenched. A love that was best expressed in books, such as the Song of Solomon. I had no conception of the blazing glory of God in his unquenchable love towards his people. Worship is an invitation to step into that glorious place of love and intimacy with Jesus.

While I am sure this does not need to be said for the vast majority of people, it is still important to note that when we are speaking of romance, passion, and intimacy, it is important that we never imply concepts of human sexuality into the mix of those words.

What does worship look like in heaven? What will we experience throughout all eternity in the manifest glory of God? To a certain degree, we are all incapable of engaging with or answering these questions. We are like congenitally blind people trying to describe color or a person who is born with absolute deafness trying to describe a Beethoven symphony. What we do know, and what scripture clearly communicates to us, is that throughout all eternity we will engage in worship in the beauty of holiness. We will live and dwell in the glory of God and his presence.

"In His presence is fullness of joy; at His right hand are pleasures forevermore" (Psalm 16:11, NKJV).

To what degree, or to what measure can we step into an experience of that same glory right here, and now upon the Earth?

I believe that it is potentially possible. The church is on a journey in worship, which is both glorious and terrifying. We have gone on a journey, where in the first stage we were singing songs about God. In this place, worship focuses on us communicating ideas, concepts, and theological truths about God, and singing them, sometimes to each other. There is a second stage of worship where we are singing to God. We are addressing our love, our worship, and our glory to him as a person. In the first stage, we sing "Look what the Lord has done;" in the second stage, we sing, "I love you, Lord, and I lift my voice." I believe this journey, though, has not yet finished. There is another stage where we move from singing about God to singing to God, and then we move to a place where we are literally singing with him. A place where we are absolutely one in intimacy joined with him. There is a place where we no longer even need a song.

"When Solomon's temple was dedicated, the glory of the Lord descended and filled the room. The Bible said that the priests were no longer able to stand in minister because of the weight of the manifest glory of God in the temple. (1 Kings 8:11, NKJV) I believe that before Jesus returns, we, the people of God (the temple of the Holy Spirit), will experience that same glory. I believe the Lord is leading the church to a place where we will no longer need a song, a worship band, a light show, or a smoke machine. When we are standing in the glory, and holiness of God's presence, there is no more work to be done. We have arrived in Christ Jesus.

This is our goal. This is our destination. There is no higher joy or pleasure on planet Earth, than being in the manifest presence of God. Worship is an invitation to move into that presence. Worship is our connection point from earth to heaven.

"God inhabits the praises of His people" (Psalm 22:3, NKJV).

How can we learn to enter such an experience of worship? I believe there are several keys that will help us on this journey. This is not a formula or a recipe, but there are principles of worship that are clearly outlined in the Bible. It is important that we come to God, in God's way, not in our own way. This is the basic lesson of Cain and Abel (Genesis 4:35, NKJV). One man approached God in God's prescribed manner with blood; the other brought before the Lord the excellence of his own labor, handiwork, and performance. I believe that in the days and years to come, the challenge that is set before the church in the West will be that of simplicity. Our goals should be that of simplicity. Our mission is to strip away all of the unnecessary things that get in the way of worship. Our intention should be to realize that we are the waiters in the restaurant; we are not the meal. The presence of God is the meal. Everything we do should simply be to get out of the way and make Jesus the center of everything. I believe we are going to see a revolution in simplicity and worship that will be glorious. We make up in entertainment what we lack in power. The more that the manifest glory of God is in the room, the less we will substitute brass for gold (Isaiah 2:20, NKJV).

"I believe that the perfect model for worship is found in the Old Testament experience of the temple. When God called Moses to walk up Mount Sinai and enter into His presence, God showed Moses the heavenly Temple, with the glory of God dwelling. God then commissioned Moses to make an earthly tent or tabernacle that would represent the model he had seen in heaven. 'See that you do all things according to the heavenly model' (Hebrews 8:5, NKJV).

To express this in simple terms, the tabernacle contained three areas:

THE OUTER COURT
THE INNER COURT
THE HOLY OF HOLIES

Each of these three areas contains specific items that were like stepping stones on the journey of the children of Israel in worship.

THE OUTER COURT

Altar of Burnt Offerings: This was a large bronze altar where sacrifices, including burnt offerings, were made. It stood prominently in the outer court and was central to the sacrificial system.

Bronze Laver: This was a large basin made of bronze used by the priests for ritual washing. Before entering the tabernacle or engaging in any sacred duties, the priests would wash their hands and feet here.

THE INNER COURT

Table of Showbread: This table held twelve loaves of bread, representing the twelve tribes of Israel, and was placed on the north side of the Holy Place. The bread was replaced weekly and was eaten only by the priests.

Golden Lamp-stand (Menorah): A golden lamp-stand with seven branches, symbolizing the light of God's presence. It was placed opposite the table of showbread on the south side of the Holy Place and was kept continually burning by the priests.

Altar of Incense: Positioned in front of the veil that separated the Holy Place from the Most Holy Place, this altar was where incense was burned twice daily by the priests. It symbolized the prayers of the people ascending to God.

THE HOLY OF HOLIES

Ark of the Covenant: This was the most sacred object in the entire tabernacle or temple. Made of acacia wood overlaid with gold, it housed the stone tablets inscribed with the Ten Commandments, a golden pot of manna, and Aaron's rod that budded. The Ark symbolized God's presence among His people, and only the high priest could enter the Holy of Holies, and that only once a year on the Day of Atonement.

Each of these three stages is comparable to stages of worship that we go through on our journey into the holy presence of God. In the same way that our body (the temple of the Holy Spirit) is made up of three parts: body, soul, spirit. These three parts of our humanity also relate to the three stages of worship.

THE OUTER COURT WORSHIP

The Outer Court relates to praise and celebration. The outer court relates much more to worship with our physical body. In this beginning stage of worship, we celebrate who God is and what he has done for us. We remember the salvation from the power of sin that brought us into the freedom of Christ Jesus. This is a place where we celebrate, we dance, we raise our hands.

"We enter into His Courts with Thanksgiving and praise" (Psalm 100:4, NKJV).

THE INNER COURT WORSHIP

The inner court is where we worship God for his person. The

inner court relates much more to worshiping God with the inner part of our being. Whereas in the outer court, we sing about God's characteristics and what he has done, in the inner court, we sing to him as a person. Rather than demonstrative celebration, this is the place for emotional worship. In the inner court, we bow down before him. In the inner court, we pour out the sacrifice of our love and emotions upon his feet.

HOLY OF HOLIES WORSHIP

As we go through the other two stages of worship, there is a place where the Holy Spirit will lead us into the holy of holies. If the outer court relates to our body, and the inner court relates to our soul. Then the holy of holies is truly the place where we worship God with our spirit.

"God is spirit, and those who worship him must worship him in spirit and in truth" (John 4:24, NKJV).

The inner court is the place where the glory of God dwells, the place where we worship the beauty of holiness, the place where the manifest, glorious presence of God is revealed. In the inner court, we abide with him. There is no work to do, no sacrifice to make, we are in the presence of the great I AM. (Exodus 3:14, NKJV).

"Be still, and know that I am God" (Psalm 46:10, NKJV).

If we want to learn to successfully come and worship in that place with consistency and ease, then it is vital that we embrace the following five principles found in scripture:

* * *

THE BLOOD OF JESUS

The first step to engage in God's presence is always found in our right standing with him. It was sin that removed us from God's presence, and it is the blood of Jesus, and the blood of Jesus alone that opens the way back into the holy place.

"Having boldness to come into the holy place by the blood of the Lamb" (Hebrews 10:19, NKJV).

The greatest enemy of worship, and the greatest hindrance to entering into God's presence, is both sin and the consciousness of sin. It is vital that we learn to establish our hearts in righteousness. And that comes alone through faith in the blood of Jesus. I would encourage every believer to get a list of the Bible verses that speak on the blood of Jesus and learn to confess and proclaim these over our own lives (in the first person) by faith. Until we know in the depths of our soul that we are righteous in our before God, then we will never come with confidence and boldness into his presence. There are many Christians who have repented of sin, but have not removed their own sense of shame and their own consciousness of sin from their souls. It is vital that we grow in this area and learn to step into our standing in the righteousness of Jesus Christ.

1. Romans 5:9 "Much more then, having now been justified by His blood, we shall be saved from wrath through Him."

2. Ephesians 1:7 "In Him we have redemption through His blood, the forgiveness of sins, according to the riches of His grace."

* * *

3. Colossians 1:20 "and by Him to reconcile all things to Himself, by Him, whether things on earth or things in heaven, having made peace through the blood of His cross."

4. Hebrews 9:14 "how much more shall the blood of Christ, who through the eternal Spirit offered Himself without spot to God, cleanse your conscience from dead works to serve the living God?"

5. Hebrews 9:22 "And according to the law almost all things are purified with blood, and without shedding of blood there is no remission."

6. Hebrews 10:19 "Therefore, brethren, having boldness to enter the Holiest by the blood of Jesus,"

7. 1 Peter 1:1819 "knowing that you were not redeemed with corruptible things, like silver or gold, from your aimless conduct received by tradition from your fathers, but with the precious blood of Christ, as of a lamb without blemish and without spot."

8. Revelation 1:5 "and from Jesus Christ, the faithful witness, the firstborn from the dead, and the ruler over the kings of the earth. To Him who loved us and washed us from our sins in His own blood,"

THE WORD OF GOD

There is an amazing key when we learn to worship based upon the word of God. I would suggest to you that, rather than singing simply emotional pop songs to Jesus, we need to fill our

111

praise with the words of scripture. God's word is powerful, and when we use the word of God to pray and praise, it will produce explosive results in our lives. "Faith comes by hearing and hearing by the word of God" (Romans 10:17, NKJV). When our praise is filled with the words of God, then our praise is filled with faith.

THE SACRIFICE OF PRAISE

There is a principle behind worship that we have often missed in Western Christianity. That is the principle of the sacrifice of praise. "Let us offer into God the sacrifice of praise, that is the fruit of lips confessing to His name" (Hebrews 13:15, NKJV).

A sacrifice is simply something that is costly to the giver. In 2 Samuel 32, David is called upon to make a sacrifice to the Lord. David's companion at the time offers David his field, his thrashing floor, his animal, and his knife to make a sacrifice. David makes a startling declaration that we can learn from. David says, "Shall I offer unto God a sacrifice that cost me nothing?" (2 Samuel 32:24, NKJV).

It is possible to come into a church service and listen to the sacrifice of praise that is given from others. God wants you to offer him something that is costly to you. Mary of Bethany poured at the feet of Jesus a sacrifice that was costly to her (one year's wages) (John 12:3, NKJV). I believe that when we come before God, it is essential to pour out at the feet of Jesus a sacrificial offering of worship. Then the glory of God will fill the house, and indeed our lives.

VULNERABILITY

There is an aspect of worship that some will struggle with. I have noticed that this is often true of men in worship, and that is the subject of vulnerability before the Lord. When we look at worship solely through the lens of celebration and triumph, it is easy for us to feel safe and secure in our celebration. When the Holy Spirit is calling us into intimacy, he is also calling us into vulnerability. There is a glorious place of insecurity before the Lord where we find our security in him, and in him alone. In this realm of worship, we allow the spirit of God to remove the walls, and the masks with which we protect ourselves.

"We all, beholding as in a mirror the glory of the Lord, are being changed into the same image" (2 Corinthians 3:18, NKJV).

If this is an area you struggle with, ask the Lord to help you. We cannot bring any pretense or image before the Lord in worship. To worship the Lord, in truth means to be real with him. We will experience the reality of God to the measure that we are being real with ourselves.

BEING LED BY THE HOLY SPIRIT

Finally, if we want our worship to move forward into the glory of God, then we need to learn to be led by the Spirit of the Lord in our worship. There is something in our human makeup that whenever we have done something once successfully, we tend to think we can reproduce the same results by doing the same thing over and over. God does not want us to have confidence in our understanding of worship. God does not want us to have confidence in our ability to enter into his presence. God wants us to have confidence in the blood of Jesus, and the leading of the Holy Spirit.

In the Old Testament, God required that the priests wear a linen ephod, a priestly garment, and also come into his presence with bare feet. (Exodus 28:42, NKJV). The linen ephod would speak of a garment with no sweat. God would not require any of men's efforts to come into his presence. The priests coming in barefooted spoke about the sensitivity in their walk before the Lord. The soles of our feet are a very sensitive part of our body. We all need to learn to be led by the Holy Spirit in worship. There are times when He will emphasize a particular part of worship. We need worship leaders who will prepare and do the due diligence in terms of organization. In spite of that, we need worship leaders who will also be willing to throw aside all of the preplanned ideas about where God is taking a congregation and learn to be led by the Spirit. If we will practice reliance and vulnerability in the leading of the Holy Spirit, we will learn to come to God's presence with confidence, boldness, and wonder.

Take some time to think through the questions for reflection, and write down a vision for how you desire to live your life in terms of worship.

How does God wish you to live out your private worship life? What does it mean to be a committed member of a community of worshipers ushering in the glory of God?

Questions for Meditation

- *Are there ideas and scripts about this area of your life that heaven wants to rewrite in this season?*

- *What are the challenges you have in relation to this subject? Describe them as past, defeated, and nailed to the cross.*

- *What is the Lord displacing in your life? What new thing does He want to replace the old with?*

- *How does God define my identity?*

- *Describe the relationship that God is calling you to have with Him in this area.*

- *If God were saying "Yes and Amen", what would your request be?*

- *What would living in complete freedom, joy, and victory look like?*

- *What promise is God speaking over you in this season? What are the promises He is calling you to declare back to Him?*

- *What would transformation look like under your present circumstances?*

- *What would it take for you to develop a mindset, a lifestyle, a persona of fullness as a way of life?*

- *How are you called to minister to others?*

Chapter Eight

The Holy Spirit

Welcome to the Day of the Holy Spirit. We are living in the most glorious season on planet Earth. These are the days of Joel, the days of the outpouring of the Holy Spirit. There is no idea more dangerous in Christianity than the idea that Jesus died, paid the price for our sins, and then went to heaven, leaving us with just a book. Instead, the New Testament says Jesus ascended on high and poured out his Spirit on all flesh. In Numbers 11, we read a fascinating story in the life of Moses. Moses, on the advice of his father-in-law Jethro, ordained 70 elders to work under him and support him in the work of shepherding the people of Israel. Despite having the system in place, Moses was still frustrated and crushed under the workload of shepherding God's people.

Moses cried out to the Lord in his frustration, and God shows him the root of the problem. The problem is that these men are good men who have a heart to serve Moses, but they have not been anointed with the power of the Holy Spirit in their lives to enable them to do the task that is set before them. This is so true of the evangelical church in the world today. The Lord commands Moses to take the 70 elders outside of the camp, and the Lord tells Moses that he will pour out, on the elders, the spirit and the same anointing that is upon Moses. Moses gathers the elders and proceeds to take them outside of the camp, and the Spirit of God falls upon them, and they all begin to prophesy. The Bible tells of two elders who are missing from the group: one called Eldad and another called Medad. When the group has departed, Joshua alone is left to tidy up the area they used. When Eldad and Medad come to the gathering, after everybody has departed, the Spirit of the Lord falls upon them as well, and they begin to prophesy.

Joshua, in his annoyance and frustration, comes to Moses and asks Moses to forbid these two men from prophesying. We get a glorious glimpse of the heart of God, breaking out through the heart of Moses in Moses' response to Joshua. Moses replies to Joshua:

"Are you zealous for my sake? Oh, that all the Lord's people were prophets and that the Lord would put His Spirit upon them!" (Numbers 11:29 NKJV)

In the Old Testament, only a very few select people were anointed or filled with the Holy Spirit. Essentially, this came down to three categories of ministry: prophets, priests, and kings. Under the old covenant, God would put His Spirit upon a man or a woman for a specific work of ministry. We see in this passage the heart of Moses yearning for the day when God would pour His Spirit out on all flesh. Moses' cry is for every child, every man, and every woman, every senior citizen of the nation to be filled to overflowing with the power of the Holy Spirit. This is exactly what happened on the day of Pentecost. God poured out His Spirit on all flesh. For the first time in human history, the ability to be filled with and overflowing with the power and presence of God was made available to everyone who would receive God's gift.

"And it shall come to pass afterward
That I will pour out My Spirit on all flesh;
Your sons and your daughters shall prophesy,
Your old men shall dream dreams,
Your young men shall see visions.
And also on My menservants and on My maidservants
I will pour out My Spirit in those days." (Joel 2:2829 NKJV).

God is looking for a Spiritfilled Church. This is the only kind of Church that is acceptable to Him, and it is the only kind of Christian life that works. We cannot live the Christian life in our own strength or in our own power.

"Not by might nor by power, but by My Spirit,"
Says the Lord of hosts. (Zechariah 4:6 NKJV).

I believe the church needs to undergo a reformation and rethink what it truly means to be filled and overflowing with the power of the Holy Spirit. There is a glorious experience called the baptism of the Holy Spirit that is available to each and every believer, and in the coming passages, we will explore how to receive this experience and live in, and live out, a life filled with the presence of God.

I believe there are two main challenges facing the Western church today regarding the subject:

The first challenge is that there are still many believers living in the first chapter of the book of Acts. Believers who have truly been born again of the Holy Spirit but have never stepped into a vital, real baptism of the Holy Spirit. Especially in the United States, for many historical reasons, churches have shied away from teaching the Bible on the subject.

There is a second challenge that faces many of the Pentecostal, Charismatic churches. Most believers within these churches have received the experience of the baptism of the Holy Spirit, and yet for many of these believers, that remains an experience that happened to them once in life rather, than an ongoing life of being constantly filled and refilled. Many of these believers have a true testimony of being baptized in the Holy Spirit, but they do not have an ongoing testimony of His power in their lives. Whichever camp we may find ourselves in, and whatever our theological background, we need to embrace the humility necessary to allow God to challenge and reform our current thinking. Humility is a powerful tool in the life of the believer. When we come before the Lord with hungry and humble hearts, we posture ourselves to receive more of His grace and to enlarge the place of the tent of our faith.

"Humble yourselves in the sight of the Lord, and He will lift you up." (James 4:10 NKJV).

What is our ultimate vision for the Spiritfilled life? The answer is found in the life of Jesus. Jesus is our Savior and also our example. We are called to walk just as He walks.

Jesus said, "I can of Myself do nothing," and then He did everything. Everything that Jesus did, He did by the power of the Holy Spirit. The further we move into ministry, the more we need to move into dependence on the power and presence of the Holy Spirit. God does not anoint us and gift us to make us independent from Him. In the natural world, we wish to raise our children to come to maturity and independence. In the kingdom of God, we can measure our maturity by measuring our dependence upon the Lord Himself.

Jesus lived for 30 years as the perfect Son of God, in righteousness and full fellowship with His Father, and yet He performed no miracles whatsoever. At age 30, He was baptized in the Holy Spirit, which was the doorway into His ministry. If Jesus needed the power of the Holy Spirit for ministry, how much more do we?

What does it mean to be baptized in the Holy Spirit? The baptism in the Holy Spirit is a definite experience from God, where the believer is filled to overflowing with the Spirit of the living God. At the new birth, the moment of our conversion, God's Spirit comes to dwell in us. And yet the Bible speaks about a subsequent experience, being filled with power for ministry. It is possible to receive this experience at the moment of one's conversion, but it is equally biblical, and in my experience, more common, to receive this experience subsequent to a salvation encounter with Jesus. Most of the accounts of people being baptized in the Holy Spirit in the book of Acts happened after the conversion experience. I believe there is a onetime baptism in the Holy Spirit that is the doorway into this experience, but there is also an ongoing life of being filled with the Holy Spirit.

"And do not be drunk with wine, in which is dissipation; but be filled with the Spirit." (Ephesians 5:18 NKJV).

* * *

How do we receive this experience?

In the early days of the Pentecostal movement, there was a teaching that one would come before the Lord and wait, or tarry, to be filled with the Holy Spirit. This teaching was based on Jesus' commandment to the apostles to wait in Jerusalem until they received the infilling of the Holy Spirit. While Jesus correctly asked the disciples to wait for the Holy Spirit, we no longer need to wait as the he has already been given or poured out. Rather than asking God to pour the Spirit upon us, we need to believe, as the Scripture says, that the Holy Spirit is already poured out on the Earth. We need then to receive the gift that God has already given. We receive the Holy Spirit and His baptism in our lives purely by faith.

"Therefore He who supplies the Spirit to you and works miracles among you, does He do it by the works of the law, or by the hearing of faith?" (Galatians 3:5 NKJV).

Often when people are baptized in the Holy Spirit, they experience a dramatic encounter with God: overflowing emotions, tears, laughter, an experience of drunkenness, or overpowering peace. While it is valid and biblical to experience these things, we should never judge what we have received from God based on a physical or emotional experience. We receive the Holy Spirit by faith and by faith alone. Faith means that we believe the promise of God in His written Word.

If you have never had this experience, I encourage you right now to come before the Lord, to ask Him to fill you with the Holy Spirit, and believe that you have received, at the moment you pray.

* * *

"Therefore I say to you, whatever things you ask when you pray, believe that you receive them, and you will have them." (Mark 11:24 NKJV).

You can now thank him baptizing you into the Holy Spirit, without waiting for any feeling, sensation, or even any spiritual gift to prove that you have received this experience. Base your experience on faith alone.

What is the role of speaking in tongues in the life of the believer? I believe that God wants every Christian to speak in tongues. I have never met one person who desired this gift, who did not easily receive it from the Lord. Sometimes people needed some help and instruction to get over their own personal hindrances in this area. Both biblically, and in the experience of hundreds of millions of people all over the world, the gift of tongues seems to be the first gift that the believer can step into after having been filled with the Holy Spirit. This is not necessarily the case. In the book of Acts, we see examples of people prophesying as well as speaking in tongues, but everybody we see having received the baptism in the Spirit, received the gift of speaking in tongues. Speaking in tongues is a glorious way of praying and communicating with God. The apostle Paul said, "I thank my God I speak with tongues more than you all." (1 Corinthians 14:18 NKJV). The gift of tongues is like a gateway gift into the other gifts. As one develops and learns to flow in this gift, it seems to open up a doorway to all of the other gifts. I encourage you to pray in tongues much, often, and frequently.

How can we build a Spirit-filled life?

* * *

So, we have seen that when we are born again, we are born of the Spirit of God. When we are baptized in the Holy Spirit, we are anointed and filled with the Spirit's presence. How then can we stay in that place of being full and overflowing with the Holy Spirit? It is interesting that in the Bible, every word or analogy that is used of the Holy Spirit is something in motion: wind, fire, flowing water. The Holy Spirit is referred to as a rushing river, but never a static pond. Imagine if I were to pour a glass of cool, refreshing water and hand it to you. And then, instead of you drinking it, you would put it on a shelf in your office, and it would sit there for days, weeks, months, or even several years. If after years you reached out for a refreshing, cool drink of water and drank from the cup, you would probably be disgusted, disappointed, and possibly quite ill. The water I had given you several years earlier was indeed healthy and refreshing. As we all know, water is never designed or meant to be left in a static place for a long period of time. Inactivity is death to water. You may buy the most expensive bottle of mineral water, in a designer bottle and label, and leave it standing on the shelf for a long time; it will eventually go bad. God designed water to be something that would flow.

In the same way, there are many in the Pentecostal and Charismatic church circles who can tell you about a glorious experience they had with the Holy Spirit back in the days of Azusa Street, the healing revival of the 50s, the charismatic movement, the word of faith movement, Toronto, Brownsville, and on we go. And when you get near them, you find refreshing water. But from their innermost being does not spring forth the river of living water. It is not that their initial baptism in the Holy Spirit was not valid. Rather, it is simply that they have allowed what once happened to them to become a static experience in life.

"Jesus stood and cried out, saying, 'If anyone is thirsty, let him come to Me and drink. He who believes in Me, as the Scripture said, 'From his innermost being will flow rivers of living water.'" (John 7:3738 NKJV).

How then can we stay filled with the Spirit of the Lord?

The answer to this question is so simple that many of us have missed it. Many years ago, the Lord spoke to me and said, "Graham, if you want an outpouring, then pour out." I believe the only way to stay full of the Holy Spirit is to live in a place, to embrace a lifestyle where we are constantly being emptied. In Ephesians 5, the apostle Paul encourages believers to be filled with the Spirit. He uses the present continual tense. This verse could well be translated, "Be, being, filled with the Holy Spirit."

"And do not be drunk with wine, in which is dissipation; but be filled with the Spirit." (Ephesians 5:18 NKJV).

If every day we will pour out, then every day God will pour in. If every day we will empty ourselves, then every day God will fill us. The way to live a Spiritfilled life is to live "poured out" life.

How to live a poured out life?

"Therefore do not be unwise, but understand what the will of the Lord is. And do not be drunk with wine, in which is dissipation; but be filled with the Spirit, speaking to one another in psalms and hymns and spiritual songs, singing and making melody in your heart to the Lord, giving thanks always for all things to God the Father in the name of our Lord Jesus Christ." (Ephesians 5:1720 NKJV).

In this passage, the apostle Paul tells us not to be unwise, but to understand God's will for our lives. Paul then goes on to clearly spell out exactly what God's will is for our lives: that we live full and filled with the Holy Spirit. How do we do this in practical ways? How can we learn to pour out so that God will pour in?

Here are four practical ways that I have learned to effectively pour out from your innermost being and allow God to pour in:

HUNGER

God loves hungry individuals. Hungry individuals are sometimes messy eaters. Nevertheless, God cherishes it when we approach Him and pour out our innermost selves. We will receive the fullness of God in accordance with our hunger for Him. It is crucial to understand that when we speak of hungering for God, we are not describing a scenario where we are crying out for more of God and He is withholding His presence or power from us. God has already bestowed upon us everything in Christ. God has already poured out the fullness of His Spirit on the day of Pentecost. When we talk about hunger, we are not petitioning God for more, and God is not refusing. Rather, the perspective on hunger is that many things in our lives—our own choices, priorities, desires, and agendas—occupy our lives. There is potency in approaching the Lord and declaring our hunger beforehand, asking Him to assist us in pushing everything out of the way that would obstruct the flow of His Spirit in our lives. Hunger is not an emotion. Hunger can evoke an emotion. There are times when we may feel hungry, but we can always opt to be hungry as a direct act of our will. When you proclaim before the Lord, "Lord, I am hungry for You," the feelings and sensations of hunger will ensue.

One of the most effective methods I have ever found for accomplishing this is to kneel and read aloud Psalm 42. When David speaks of thirsting after God as the deer pants for water on a hot day, it is a prophetic prayer that we can utter, and I assure you God will respond.

WORSHIP

One of the primary methods we utilize to pour out from our innermost being (and thus, God will pour back in) is through worship. We were created for worship, destined for worship, and it is only through worship that we discover our true identity. Worship is not merely singing a song or attending a church service. Worship is the act of pouring out from our innermost being as an active sacrifice before the Lord. Consider Mary of Bethany, who approached Jesus and took her most valuable possession, a jar of precious ointment. (John 12:3) She did not deposit it in the offering basket or dedicate it to His ministry. She did not, to the consternation of Judas, donate it to the poor. Instead, she took this most precious resource and poured it out at the feet of Jesus in an act of worship. What a magnificent image of us pouring out from our innermost being. While it is wonderful to gather with thousands of other believers in an arena with amazing music, and sing praises to God, there is something even more glorious about a solitary saint who gathers in the secret place when no one sees, no one observes, no one is looking, and kneels, raises their hands in the air, and pours out a song of praise to the living God. When someone does this, the Father who sees in secret will reward them openly. (Matthew 6:6)

PRAYING IN TONGUES

Another method, by which we can learn to pour out from our innermost being, is through the supernatural gift of praying in tongues. As previously mentioned, the gift of tongues is one of the initial gifts we experience when filled with the Spirit. It is disheartening to note that many Christians speak in tongues when first filled with the Spirit and view it as a sign or proof of the Spirit's presence in their lives, yet many Christians do not speak in tongues regularly. Jesus said, "Out of your belly will flow rivers of living water," speaking of the Holy Spirit who would be poured out. (John 7:38).

When we pray in tongues, we are tapping into the life of the Spirit within us. We are not praying from our minds but from our spirit in the most personal manner. Isaiah spoke of the experience of speaking in tongues that would come upon the future people of God in Isaiah 28:11, "With stammering lips and another tongue, I will speak to this people. This is the rest. This is the refreshing."

It can be challenging for younger believers to learn to persevere in speaking in tongues. Often, there is an element of warfare surrounding this gift. Satan opposes it when we speak in tongues, and there is a part of our natural flesh which opposes it as well. Frequently, when a young believer begins to speak in tongues, they can become distracted or disheartened. We must learn to pray with a decision of our will, and also in faith. Sometimes, we have learned to associate the gift of tongues with a euphoric or supernatural experience. While this is valid, we should never gauge the effectiveness of the gift of tongues solely by the personal experience it provides. I would encourage you to learn to pray in tongues by setting a timer, for instance, 10 minutes initially. Make the decision to pray in tongues, to pour out from your innermost being to your creator, and do not allow yourself to judge whether this worked solely on the basis of your feelings or emotions. I assure you, if you persevere and develop an ongoing habit of praying in tongues, this will lead you into a new realm of fullness in the Holy Spirit and also edify and build up your inner self. (1 Corinthians 14:4)

MINISTRY TO OTHERS

Another significant method by which we can pour out from our innermost being is through ministry to others. Primarily, in the ministry of intercession. It is possible to pray for others simply with our minds, and this is both valid and effective. But there is also a place of intercession where we pray from our innermost being. The apostle Paul describes this in Romans 8 when he speaks of praying with groans and supplications from the innermost heart. (Romans 8:26). When we pray for others, also known as intercessory prayer, we are pouring out from the Holy Spirit within us. Quite literally, the Holy Spirit is praying in and through us, and we are uttering Spirit-inspired prayers. When we approach the Lord with love for others, we are tapping into the reservoir of life within us. Again, the same principle applies: as we pour out, God will pour in.

* * *

We can also pour out of the Spirit within us as we minister to others: as we pray for the sick, as we prophesy, as we love, and as we serve. Whenever we minister under the anointing, we are drawing from the Holy Spirit within us. As a traveling minister, I would often speak in 8 to 10 churches a week. Usually, after speaking, would have a prayer line of sometimes hundreds of people who came forward for ministry. In one sense, it is physically tiring to preach for an hour, and then spend two hours standing ministering to people. Despite this, I have discovered that whenever I was drawing from the Spirit of God within me, I was being refreshed myself. I have learned that after several hours of ministry, which can be tiring and demanding, I am usually alive and overflowing with the power of God. As I poured out, heaven poured in.

When Elisha the prophet came to the widow who only had one small jar of oil, he asked her to gather as many empty vessels as possible. The lady obeyed and filled the house with empty vessels. The prophet then instructed the lady to take the one small jar of oil that she had and pour it out. And as she poured out, heaven poured in. (2 Kings 4:34 NKJV) We cannot gauge or quantify our measure of the Spirit of the Lord. It is easy to look at yourself and think or feel that you are not very anointed. Do not assess or measure your experience of the Spirit of God within you. Instead, go and find as many empty vessels as possible and pour out. Remember, to live a life of outpouring, we need to live a life of pouring out.

Questions for Meditation

- *Are there ideas and scripts about this area of your life that heaven wants to rewrite in this season?*
- *What are the challenges you have in relation to this subject? Describe them as past, defeated, and nailed to the cross.*
- *What is the Lord displacing in your life? What new thing does He want to replace the old with?*
- *How does God define my identity?*
- *Describe the relationship that God is calling you to have with Him in this area.*
- *If God were saying "Yes and Amen", what would your request be?*
- *What would living in complete freedom, joy, and victory look like?*
- *What promise is God speaking over you in this season? What are the promises He is calling you to declare back to Him?*
- *What would transformation look like under your present circumstances?*
- *What would it take for you to develop a mindset, a lifestyle, a persona of fullness as a way of life?*
- *How are you called to minister to others?*

Chapter Nine

Kingdom Finances

"If I were a rich man,
Ya ha deedle deedle, bubba bubba deedle deedle dum.
All day long I would biddy biddy bum.
If I were a wealthy man."

What would you do if finance were no object whatsoever in your life? How would you live if you were constantly connected to God's supply? In this chapter, we are going to explore together, developing a vision for our financial and material life. I would encourage you to approach this subject with the same thoughtfulness and intention as any other topic in this book. One of the greatest temptations a Christian can face in the area of finances is not thinking about this subject too much but rather thinking of it too little.

Whether you like it or not, whether you admit it or not, this is an important part of your life. The Bible has more to say on this subject than most other topics, and yet that message has been distorted over the years. There is, within much of modern

Christianity, a tendency to look at the subject as one that is beneath us. To look down upon anybody who would speak, teach, or write about finances. We are often taught, at a subliminal level, that it is not that important or spiritual what we do in this arena. There is a concept communicated often that to talk about money and finances is not a very spiritual thing to do. I believe the opposite is true. The Bible clearly teaches that God has a defined plan for this area of our lives. I would also point out that if we do not enter into God's plan, then by default, we end up functioning in Satan's plan for our life. Satan has done a masterful job of distorting this area of our lives and bringing us into bondage.

I believe that if we were able to isolate and analyze most of our core beliefs about money, we would discover that they are extremely unbiblical and dangerous. Much of our teaching, even in modern evangelical circles, bears no relation to the Bible's teaching on finances, money, and resources. The nearest thing we can approach to God's concept of how we should live financially would probably be found in more traditional Jewish communities. Although many of these communities may not yet fully see the light on Jesus, the Messiah, and they carry much religious baggage, they often still walk in biblical principles of stewardship. There is much we could learn from those communities.

We all, as broken people, have a tendency to project our own brokenness into any subject. This is true of finance and resources as much as any other subject. I invite you as part of this book to reexamine your thoughts in the light of biblical teaching. I call you to have the courage it will require, when necessary, to be willing to discard traditional teaching that simply contradicts the principles of God's word.

"For the love of money is a root of all kinds of evil" (1 Timothy 6:10 NKJV).

As we begin to examine this subject, let us look at some foundational truths. Firstly, money has no inherent nature. Money is amoral, not immoral. That means money has no inherent virtue or vice as part of it. The issue at stake is the character or heart of the person who possesses that money. It is possible to use money for good or ill depending on the heart of the person. The Bible has much to say in terms of warning us of the dangers of greed. It is important that we grasp that greed is a heart issue, not a bank account one. It is possible to have a heart filled with greed and an empty bank account. It is equally possible to have a full bank account and a heart full of worship, generosity, and service to the kingdom of God. Religion has misquoted the verse about the love of money. Money is not the root of evil.

"The love of money is a root of evil" (1 Timothy 6:10 NKJV).

The antidote to the love of money is not the lack of money. The antidote to the love of money is the love of Jesus! The answer to a heart of greed is not found in stinginess or self deprivation. The answer to a greed filled heart is found in repentance, humility, and a life of worship. "The lamp of the body is the eye. If therefore your eye is good, your whole body will be full of light" (Matthew 6:22 NKJV).

WHY THIS IS IMPORTANT

Why is the subject so important? It is actually very easy for us to vastly underestimate the amount of time, energy, and focus we dedicate to this arena of our lives. To a large degree, we can determine the value we place on an area of our life by the amount of time and focus we give to it. If we say we love God and the things of the kingdom of God, then it is important that we are honest about how much time we give to God's kingdom in our lives.

I would suggest to you that we give more time to providing for our material needs than any other part of our life. From the time our children are young, we send them to school. The average child will begin attending school somewhere around four years of age and usually progress through high school to college, which will end anywhere around 18 to 24 years of age. Why do we educate our children? I know it is easy to reply with answers about developing brain capacity, wishing them to understand the history of the world, and all of the classical disciplines. I think if we are honest, to a very large degree, the primary reason for educating children is so they have a good career and the capacity to earn a living well in this world. Simply put, the average child in America will receive about 20 years of education with the aim of getting a job, and the goal of having a job, career, or business is to provide income for our lives.

The average adult in America will work at least 40 hours a week. In addition to this, that same person will often spend sometimes over an hour each way commuting to work, etc. In these days of technology, the Internet, communications, and

Zoom calls, many people do not even have the hard edges of a cutoff point to the working day. It is likely that you and I know many people who literally work from morning till night. My goal in saying these things is not to criticize anybody and certainly not to put a Western work ethic in a negative light. Rather, my point is simply to illustrate that the average Christian will spend much more time working than they will with family, hobbies, friends, or certainly involved in the things of God. If we claim this area of our life, that of our finances, is not that important to us, not that important to God, I believe we are deceiving ourselves. Satan loves to fill the vacuum of our focus and dictate the course of our lives.

But one of his disciples, Judas Iscariot, who was later to betray him, objected, 5 "Why wasn't this perfume sold and the money given to the poor? It was worth a year's wages." He did not say this because he cared about the poor but because he was a thief; as keeper of the money bag, he used to help himself to what was put into it. John 12:46

One of the hallmarks of religious thinking is a lack of understanding about money. Satan is the god of poverty. Judas Iscariot was offended at Mary's extravagant giving, and equally Jesus's receptivity to that giving. If Satan can handle the flow of finances in the body of Christ, then to a large degree, he can hinder the advancement of the gospel. Having traveled in ministry for many years, I've come to the conclusion that many ministers spend 80% of their time trying to raise finance to do 20% of what God has called them to do. I do not believe this was ever God's plan from the beginning. If we are to become the people God plans and purposes us to be, it is important that we break the curse of poverty around the body of Christ and step into a place of freedom and blessing.

Once, several years ago, I was attending a pastors' luncheon with around 12 ministers present. When it came time to pay for the check, many of these pastors began quibbling about who would pay for what. Somebody made the comment that they had only had water with the meal and did not want to simply divide the check equally between those present. I sat at the outside of this conversation observing with an equal mixture of amusement and disgust. Suddenly, two great revelations came upon me: Firstly, I realized I could not afford to be part of this conversation. I realize I could not afford to participate in this kind of discussion as a child of God. The second revelation was that I could afford to pay for the whole meal, for everybody present, that was within my gift, which I then proceeded to do.

I want to suggest to you the same thing is true for you. It is dangerous for you and I to allow the thinking of religion to enter into our hearts. We cannot afford to do so. We are called to a life of freedom, where we are blessed to be a blessing to others.

When God originally created mankind and the Garden of Eden, he had planned and provided for everything they would ever need. They were born into a kingdom of supply. They never related to any sense of lack or struggle to supply their needs. God had foreseen every need they would ever have and abundantly supplied for that need. They were called to attend the garden and participate in its upkeep, but the concept of work, earning one's living through the sweat of one's brow only came after sin and the fall (Genesis 2:89 NKJV). God planned for man to be completely independent of need. We see this in God's original plan and purpose for creation at the beginning of the Bible, and we see the same thing at the end of the Bible in the New Jerusalem. In eternity future, not one person will experience lack. God will provide according to his riches and glory in Christ Jesus. (Philippians 4:19 NKJV). This was God's original plan and design for mankind. It was only through the fall of man that we fell into need, and Jesus fully paid the price that we may come back into the garden at the Cross of Calvary. How did Jesus live and what was his relation to the material world? I encourage you to be willing to challenge your preconceptions regarding this. Religion has told us about a Jesus who was poor as a church mouse, and had no possessions. Is that actually true?

I would suggest to you that if we look at the pages of the Gospels and read what they actually say, another picture will appear to us. At Jesus's birth, kings appeared bringing to him gold, frankincense, and myrrh. All the way through Jesus's life and ministry, we see one abundant truth proclaimed. Jesus lived completely free from all material need; whatever Jesus needed, God would fully supply. Whether that was a place to live, food, or money to pay his taxes, everything was abundantly supplied in the life of Jesus. We never once see Jesus living in a place of lack. When Jesus sent the original disciples out to minister, one of his practical instructions to them was not to take an offering basket, not to take a spare coat, etc. Jesus wanted to prove to the disciples that everywhere they went, they could rely on the invisible supply of God. Jesus wanted the disciples to understand that in the world of God, the provision of God would always flow.

When the disciples returned, Jesus asked them if they lacked anything on the trip. The reply was, "We lacked nothing" (Luke 22:35 NKJV). Jesus then instructed his disciples that in the future, they could take an offering bag, they could take a spare coat, etc. (Matthew 10:910 NKJV). His point was that he wanted the disciples to learn by personal experience, not simply to rely on others. God can be trusted to meet any need in any circumstance. The same is true today.

One of my heroes of the faith was the missionary Brother Andrew. Brother Andrew was famous for smuggling Bibles behind the Iron Curtain and later, helping to promote the gospel in many countries where persecution was an ongoing reality through Open Doors Ministries. In his autobiographical book, "God's Smuggler," Brother Andrew tells the story of the Bible school he attended in the UK. He recounted that in the final year of his studies, there was a test that all the Bible school students must perform before they could graduate. The school would send out students to preach all over Scotland. They had to rent halls, print flyers, invite people, organize public gospel events. At the beginning of this one month ministry, each student was given 1 pound in money, and at the end, they had to return the 1 pound. They were not allowed to request money in any way, shape, or form during the trip; they were not allowed to take any offerings or share their needs with anybody, except to the Lord in prayer. Brother Andrew refers to this as "the game of the Royal Way." He stresses that he learned more in this month than in many years of Christian walk. He learned that God can be trusted. Oh, that we could learn that same truth; our lives would be transformed.

Jesus lived a life completely free from material need. The natural serves the purpose of the spiritual. We are called to have that same walk. Our goal is not to be rich. Our goal is to flourish and spend our lives in relationship with God. Our purpose is not to seek the things of this world. Our purpose is to seek first the kingdom of God and his righteousness (Matthew 6:33 NKJV), and to believe by faith that every single thing we will ever need will be added to us.

God is able to make all Grace abound towards you, so that you will have sufficiency in all things, and in turn, you will abound into every good work. (2 Corinthians 9:8 NKJV)

THE HEART OF THE MATTER

God is not remotely interested in coins, banknotes, stocks, shows, or commodities. He only cares about people and their hearts. The key to understanding biblical finance always comes down to the heart of a person.

For where your treasure is, there your heart will be also. (Matthew 6:21)

When our hearts are aligned with the plans and purposes of God, when our hearts are bathed in worship, we enter into a place where God can truly bless us.

Beloved, I pray that you may prosper in all things and be in health, just as your soul prospers. (3 John 1:2)

The challenge for every believer is to allow God to take possession of the affections of our heart. When our hearts are full of the things of God, the material realm will serve us rather than the other way around. Money is a great servant, but it is a terrible master.

BIBLICAL THINKING ABOUT MONEY

A biblical proposition of how God wants us to live regarding this.

How does God want us to live in the financial realm? God wants us to live exactly like Jesus did in this realm. I believe, and indeed, have proved in my own life and ministry, that God is able to supply every need we can ever have.

Throughout the Old Testament, there is ongoing and progressive revelation of the nature and names of God. We begin to know God as the "I am that I am" in the book of Exodus 3:14 and all the way through the history, poetry, and prophetic writings in the Old Testament. We are seeing more of who God is. When Jesus comes, he gives us the final and ultimate revelation of who God is, summed up in the ultimate name for God: "father" (Please add the Bible verse here)

God is a father. God is a good father. God is an amazing father.

If you then, being evil, know how to give good gifts to your children, how much more will your Father who is in heaven... (Matthew 7:11)

Take a moment and think how you would wish your own children to live in terms of finances. I do not think that anybody would wish children to be spoiled or greedy, but I equally do not believe that any true loving parent would wish the children to live in poverty and lack. We would want our children to appreciate the value of hard work and diligence. We would want our children to understand and appreciate the things they have and the blessings that are theirs. We would want our children to go through seasons where they learn things in life and do not always expect life to be easy, but ultimately we would want our children to be blessed, and indeed to be a blessing to those around them. I believe that is the clearly revealed will of God in His Word. (Genesis 12:12)

There is a word that is used throughout the Bible that causes unusual reactions in the minds of many believers. That word is "prosperity". As with any biblical truth or legitimate revelation, there are those who will take it too far and make an element of God's Word the only thing in God's Word. Is it true that people have preached a message of prosperity that has been abusive and greedy? Yes, I believe that can be said of some people.

I believe this is equally true of any truth or revelation that God has restored to the body of Christ. When Martin Luther had a revelation of justification by faith, he became so extreme that he wanted to remove the book of James from the Bible, because James stated that faith without works is dead. (James 2:17)

Some of the early Baptists had such a revelation of the importance of water baptism that they overemphasized its importance and believed that one could not be saved without baptism. Any truth, given overemphasis can become error. The answer to error is not to throw away truth. The answer is to come back to a true biblical understanding of the truth and the place it plays in the whole of scripture. The answer to poor teaching on biblical finance is not to ignore teaching on biblical finance.

143

During church history, many great saints like Francis of Assisi saw the greed and avarice of the Roman Catholic Church and were rightly disgusted by it. The answer was to not go to another extreme and preach a message of poverty which the Bible knows nothing of. I encourage you to come back and develop a personal vision for a financial life where the goal is not being rich, but the goal is being free. As we grow and develop in our Christian walk, we will walk through various steps of understanding regarding this truth. At times, it can seem that some of these truths can contradict each other.

The fear of the Lord is the beginning of wisdom. (Proverbs 9:10) We cannot begin a relationship with God without the fear of the Lord, but when we have experienced that fear of the Lord and come to the Lord in repentance, the Lord wants to establish us in His love and security without fear in our relationship with Him.

'Twas grace that taught my heart to fear, and grace my fears relieved.

In the gospel, Jesus says to the disciples, "I no longer call you servants, I now call you friends."(John 15:15) Is there something wrong with serving Jesus? No, we begin out of a servant relationship, but as we grow in that relationship, we move into a higher place of friendship. As a friend of God, I still serve God, but I know His heart in a way a servant would simply not.

In order to grow in our understanding and revelation of God's plan for us in this role, I believe it is necessary that we pass through five phases:

* * *

1. SACRIFICE.
2. OBEDIENCE.
3. STEWARDSHIP.
4. BLESSING.
5. INFLUENCE.

The first stage in our walk with God has always been one of sacrifice. All the way through the Bible, we see the call of God for people to leave everything and follow Him. (Luke 9:23) God calls Abraham to leave everything behind and promises him that he will be blessed in the future. (Genesis 12:1) Jesus calls all of the disciples in the same way. Jesus calls us to walk through a narrow gate and a straight way with which we can bring no baggage. (Matthew 7:14) If we are to be true disciples of Jesus, we need to be willing to leave everything behind and follow Him in that way.

There are many people who can never begin a walk with God because they are not willing to leave everything behind. When Jesus called the rich, young ruler, I believe that He had a plan and destiny for this young man, but the man was not willing to pass test number one and leave everything behind.

OBEDIENCE

When we have learned the lesson of sacrifice, leaving all behind, God will call us into a new realm of obedience. This is the place when we learn to tithe (to give 10% of our realworld income to the kingdom of God).

This is the place we learn to obey the Holy Spirit and give

145

offerings. In a strange way, it can be easier at times to be willing to give up everything for the gospel, especially at important junctures in our life, but the reality is that God calls us to ongoing obedience in giving. It is a sad reality that the

majority of Christians give far less than 10% of their actual income to the work of God. Is this because they do not love God? Or because they have not learned the lesson of obedience? They can point to times of great sacrifice in their life, but they have not yet embraced an ongoing lifelong commitment to obeying the word of God and working that out in their lives.

I believe that every Christian must learn obedience in four areas of financial giving:

Tithes (giving 10% of your real world income to your local church).

Offerings: This is what we do on top of our tithes. We should be led by our heart and the Holy Spirit in the money that we give as a freewill offering.

Giving to missions: I believe God wants everybody to have an investment in sending the gospel to those who have never heard it. This could be at the local level, or in international missions.

Giving to the poor: The Bible is clear that we will never eradicate poverty until Jesus returns, and the lion lays down with the lamb. Yet, in spite of this, we are called to give to those in need, to help those who are in lack and suffering poverty around us. We need wisdom and to be led by the Holy Spirit in the manner in which we do this. The poor are not always those whom we may judge to be poor.

STEWARDSHIP

When we have learned the lessons of sacrifice and obedience, God will begin to teach us about wisdom in the financial realm. He will instruct us through the lessons contained in the book of Proverbs. If we examine the Bible superficially, in a one-dimensional light, it can seem contradictory to talk about giving everything up for the gospel and then discussing how we manage money. I believe that God is seeking those who are willing to sacrifice everything for His kingdom. However, He is also seeking those who can grow and learn the ways of the kingdom, including how to manage money.

In this realm, we learn how to be wise, how to save, and how to emerge from debt. God is interested in us investing money and in running our lives and businesses through kingdom principles for His glory. The Bible is filled with stories of people like Daniel and Joseph, who transformed the culture around them through the principles and wisdom of God's stewardship as manifested in their generation.

BLESSING

When we have walked through some of the principles and stages of sacrifice, obedience, and learning the ways of God, God will begin to bless us in our life. Someone who is still walking in that first place of sacrifice could potentially look at somebody living a life of blessing and not understand. If our only revelation of God is that we should give up everything for the gospel, then the person walking with God's favor manifested in the financial realm can seem to contradict that principle. We have a God who calls us to blessing.

"For you know the grace of our Lord Jesus Christ, that though He was rich, yet for your sakes He became poor, that you through His poverty might become rich" (2 Corinthians 8:9 NKJV).

God wants to show and shower His goodness in your life in practical ways. I believe that God loves to bless His children. The key is, do we fall in love with the blessing, or rather with the God who gives us richly all things? The ultimate goal of blessing is that we then, in turn, will be a blessing to others.

"Now the Lord had said to Abram: 'Get out of your country, from your family and from your father's house, to a land that I will show you. I will make you a great nation; I will bless you and make your name great; and you shall be a blessing.'" (Genesis 12:1–2)

INFLUENCE

I believe there is a final state God calls us to where we walk in blessing, we are a blessing to others, but in addition to this, we use the resources of the kingdom of God to influence and expand God's kingdom and reach others.

God is looking for those who will not simply seek His blessings, but those to whom, and through whom, He will release the perfume of the savor of the knowledge of Christ. (2 Corinthians 2:14)

* * *

We are called to release the influence of the King of Kings everywhere we go. One of the primary ways God can do that is in the financial realm. I believe there is a call in the body of Christ to shift and change atmospheres and economies. There is authority in the body of Christ to break the curse of poverty off a family, a town, and a city. I believe that in the days to come, we will see the church releasing the influence of King Jesus in every realm, including the financial one.

The heart of the matter is always the matter of the heart. The key is always to let God reign as king in our hearts. When God can establish His throne and kingdom within our hearts, then the influence of King Jesus and His kingdom will be manifested around our lives.

Take some time to sit down and write a vision of how God wants you to live in the financial realm. What does it look like for you to live sacrificially? What does it look like for you to live by faith? What does it look like for you to be blessed? What does it look like for you to release the influence of the kingdom through blessing to others?

Questions for Meditation

- *Are there ideas and scripts about this area of your life that heaven wants to rewrite in this season?*

- *What are the challenges you have in relation to this subject? Describe them as past, defeated, and nailed to the cross.*

- *What is the Lord displacing in your life? What new thing does He want to replace the old with?*

- *How does God define my identity?*

- *Describe the relationship that God is calling you to have with Him in this area.*

- *If God were saying "Yes and Amen", what would your request be?*

- *What would living in complete freedom, joy, and victory look like?*

- *What promise is God speaking over you in this season? What are the promises He is calling you to declare back to Him?*

- *What would transformation look like under your present circumstances?*

- *What would it take for you to develop a mindset, a lifestyle, a persona of fullness as a way of life?*

- *How are you called to minister to others?*

Chapter Ten

Kingdom Relationships

The kingdom of God is a relational kingdom. Everything in God's kingdom functions in and through relationships. For us to live out the life that God has planned for us, we must learn to flourish in kingdom relationships. In this chapter, we will be exploring God's heart for our relationships here on Earth. Most of the challenges and difficulties we will face in this life will come through human relationships. As we walk through life, we will face satanic opposition. We will also deal with the effects of the fall in our own un-renewed minds, but the primary challenge for most of us will come through human relationships.

Human relationships can be, at the same time, both the source of incredible blessing and grace in our lives, and yet can hurt us and damage us in ways that we find hard to even understand. We are living in a world inhabited by creatures made in the image and likeness of God. We are also living in a world full of hurting and broken people. Broken people break people. Hurt people hurt people. Whether we choose to recognize that or not, we are all changed and affected by the different relationships that played a significant part in our lives. Learning to walk in forgiveness and healing towards others is vital, and also learning to build strong and graceful relationships is a powerful key to the Christian life.

There are times, for all of us, whether in major or minor ways, where we simply want to walk away from relationships. Whether that be family relationships, marriage relationships, church relationships, the same principle applies. There are moments, we will all be tempted to believe that simply not being close to people is the only way to navigate the challenge of relationships. I believe that if we can learn to see relationships through God's eyes, that we can learn to dwell in His love. It will empower us to break the power of rejection over our own lives, and also over the lives of others. So much of our thinking and understanding of human relationships have been distorted or twisted through the world's thinking. Our framework for looking at relationships has been so shaped by the thinking of the world that it can be a challenge and a process for us to learn to look at these things through the mindset of the kingdom of God.

"Do not be conformed to this world, but be transformed by the renewing of your mind" (Romans 12:2). This truth applies to relationships as much as any truth in God's word. Let us explore together how we can build a vision of kingdom relationships.

The foundation of Christianity is the connection between ourselves and God. Christianity revolves around divine connections between ourselves and other people made in God's image and likeness. Satan vehemently opposes any kind of kingdom relationship. Unity, especially among believers, which brings about a glorious triangulation, where God invades the space between those people. "For where two or three are gathered together in My name, I am there in the midst of them" (Matthew 18:20). There is a warfare and attack that is unleashed against kingdom relationships that we need to understand, be prepared for, and overcome.

God loves relationships. In the kingdom of heaven, relationships are the currency of life. The Trinity, the triune God, is all about relationships. The Father is in glorious relationship with the Son and glorious relationship with the Spirit. We sometimes think about Christianity in terms of Jesus coming to save us from our sins. That was never the goal of Christianity; the forgiveness of sins was a means to an end. Jesus came to call us into fellowship with God. God never intended anything for our relationships other than for them to be utterly glorious.

There are currently around 8 billion people on planet Earth. Every single person, without exception, is a masterpiece. Every single person on planet Earth is more beautiful, more glorious than the entire universe. Every person is priceless. Every person carries the image and the likeness of the glorious God stamped onto every part of the soul. We are called to have a glorious relationship with every single person we meet. There is a part of God in each of us that will resonate with the part of God in every other individual person in a way that can never be duplicated. God calls us into glorious relationships with him. God calls us into glorious relationships with each other.

Although that can seem like a cliché, it is an absolute truth, and every person we meet is our brother and sister. We are all the children of God, and our heavenly Father longs and desires for his children to flourish in relationship, one with another. All of us with more than one child can relate to the frustration of watching siblings squabble and fight, and all the glorious beauty when they begin to love and appreciate each other. We can get a tiny part of the heart of God when, as part we observe this and encourage and foster good relationships. In the kingdom of God, all relationships are win-win. The world functions by a win-lose system. The whole of fallen mankind is constantly trying to get an edge, win a battle, move forward, or climb a ladder over their brothers and sisters. From the very beginning with Cain and Abel (Genesis 4:8), there has been a deeply held belief in the heart of mankind that for one person to succeed, another person must lose. It is incredible to realize that it is only Christianity and the Bible which carries the concept of blessing. (Numbers 6:2426) God wants to incredibly bless each of his children, and in turn, we go and cause others to step into that same blessing. (Galatians 3:8) God wants you to win, God wants you to be a winner, God wants you to enable and empower others to succeed in his success also. That is kingdom relationship.

WHAT GOD INTENDS FOR THIS AREA OF OUR LIVES

In the early 2000s, I visited the country of Romania several times and worked with a Christian based orphanage organization, holding gospel and healing campaigns in the eastern part of that wonderful nation. I will never forget spending time with hundreds of orphans. It was deeply moving to see the deep hunger for love and affection in these children who had suffered so much rejection. In a very real sense, this is true for every single person on planet Earth. We are a planet of orphans. There are 8 billion people wandering the face of the Earth, longing for love, affection, and the blessing of the father, who brought them into this world. Through sin, shame, and rejection, we have all become spiritual outcasts. It is hard to fathom the depth of rejection that dwells in each and every human being, and there is only the unsearchable love of Jesus Christ that can heal and restore that person. (Romans 8:15)

"When we come to Jesus, a journey of healing begins on the inside of our soul. Every Christian is at a different place on that journey. Some of the healing will depend on the life they have led before coming to Christ. Some of that healing will depend on the willingness to allow the truth of God's word and the presence of God's Spirit to permeate their being and transform their inner-man. God desires that every person on planet Earth would experience and know him as Father. He desires us to have an ongoing relationship with the Holy Spirit as the Spirit of adoption, who bathes our life in the mercy and love of God. God desires that our hearts would be so marinated in God's love that we would enter into a relationship of utter acceptance and security in him."

"being rooted and grounded in love" Ephesians 3:17

"The plan of God for the church is that each individual would accept that place of love in the Father's heart. From that point, we would then begin to love one another with the love with which we have been loved." (John 13:34)

"The third step in this process is that the world would see who Jesus is when it observes the love of God between Christians." (John 13:35)

Simply put, God is looking for the citizens of Heaven (the

body of Christ) to model the relationships of heaven here upon the Earth. In the midst of a rejection, war-torn, hate-filled world, God is looking for the sons of light to wander the face of the Earth, filled with love, forgiveness, and grace for every person we meet. We have sought to communicate the gospel through intellectual argument and apologetic reasoning. This is not wrong, but it is grossly ineffective. The mission statement of the church is actually very simple: love the Lord your God with your heart, soul, mind, and strength, and then go love your neighbor as you love yourself. (Matthew 22:3739)

CALLED OUT RELATIONSHIPS AND LOAD-BEARING RELATIONSHIPS

"Now in the church that was at Antioch, there were certain prophets and teachers: Barnabas, Simeon who was called Niger, Lucius of Cyrene, Manaen who had been brought up with Herod the tetrarch, and Saul. As they ministered to the Lord and fasted, the Holy Spirit said, "Now separate to Me, Barnabas and Saul for the work to which I have called them." Then, having fasted and prayed, and laid hands on them, they sent them away." (Acts 13:13)

God intends that we love every person that we will ever meet, but we are not called to be in a specific relationship with every person that we meet. There are relationships that are initiated by happenstance. There are relationships which are initiated by attraction. There are relationships that are initiated by context, and there are relationships that are initiated and based on mutual understanding and appreciation of certain things. In addition to these, there are also relationships which are founded in heaven. There are relationships that we have, which are rooted in our past, and often have little connection with our present and our future. There are some relationships which are current, they have no connection with our past, but some will only continue for a season and not progress into our future. There are other relationships, that God can bring us into, which will find fulfillment in our future. It is important that we find these relationships.

There are relationships which God has planned for each and every one of us before the foundation of the earth. I call these "called-out relationships." In Acts 13, we see a group of people who love God, who are full of the Holy Spirit, and who desire to know God's plan and purpose for their lives. In this passage, the Lord is creating and calling out a relationship upon the Earth, which already existed in His heart and purpose. The Lord spoke about bringing together Barnabas and Saul (Paul), and releasing them into one. Two separate people who will both share one purpose from heaven. I believe that God has planned relationships in heaven for every one of His children. We may know and be acquainted with a lot of people, but I believe there are specific people God calls us to be yoked together with for the plans and purposes of the kingdom of God. I think it is important and vital that we learn to discern these relationships and step into, and indeed cultivate them.

These relationships have grace. These are relationships where the sum total is greater than the separate parts. When two people are called together by God, there is an incredible power that is released in their joint relationship.

"One will put a thousand to flight, two will put ten thousand to flight." (Deuteronomy 32:30)

* * *

The Holy Spirit knows our past, our present, and a future. If we will learn the daily discipline of leaning, not on our own understanding, and allowing him to guide our paths, he can lead us into the things that we will need in our future.

There are relationships that are peripheral to our lives, and there are relationships that are "load-bearing." These are the relationships upon which the structure of our life in God is built, relationships that will support the weight of the things that God will call us to, and call us to carry in life. If we simply choose and base our relationships upon mutual affection, context, or superficial preferences, we will usually miss these relationships.

When I was a teenager, I worked for a season for the Assemblies of God church planting department in the UK. As part of this work, I traveled around different areas of the UK and helped plant new churches. There was once a time when I was around 18 years of age that I was working in London for a few weeks. One day I was invited to participate in a ministers' prayer breakfast, which turned out to be a pivotal moment in my life. I was attending a meeting with around 20 pastors and church leaders, and it seemed to me that most of them were asleep. It was a really boring prayer meeting. Suddenly, I looked up and saw a man I had never met staring at me, and at that moment, the Holy Spirit within my heart stirred. This man came over to me and asked if I would have a cup of coffee with him after the prayer meeting. During that coffee, he explained to me that he was a Canadian evangelist, just visiting London for a couple of weeks to minister in churches. He said to me that during the meeting, he had noticed me, and that the Lord had spoken to him, telling him that he should help me in my journey of ministry.

After one cup of coffee, he invited me to come and work with him, and he became instrumental in my journey into full time ministry in many important ways. That was not a friendship or relationship I was looking for, but it became a "load-bearing" relationship in my life.

I have had several such instances over the years. In the early 2000s while living in France, the Lord told me to fly over to America for two weeks, and the only event of any import during that two weeks was the fact that I met one pastor at a gas station. That pastor later invited me to speak in his church, which turned out to be one of the largest churches in New England. The day I arrived to speak at that pastor's church, I was invited to minister in a church in Sturbridge, Massachusetts, which is now the church I lead as my home base.

HOW CAN WE RECOGNIZE THESE RELATIONSHIPS?

The key to recognizing these relationships is to have a heart set on the affections of the Father. When we live a life bathed in worship, there is an aligning that takes place between our hearts and the heart of heaven. Instead of learning to "know" no man after the flesh, (2 Corinthians 5:16) we ought to learn to know somebody after the spirit.

God does not see as man sees. Man looks at the outward appearance, but God looks at the heart. (1 Samuel 16:7)

We should learn to look at people through the eyes of heaven.
We should learn to look at people through the eyes of promise.

We should learn to look at people and come back into our relationship with the Lord and say, "Lord, what are you saying about this person?" When we practice seeing people through the heart of God, it will become easy to recognize these relationships.

Life in the spirit is about learning to move from assumed relationships to defined relationships. There is a place in every relationship where we are simply getting to know somebody. There is a place in every relationship where a minimal level of commitment is appropriate. There comes a time in a relationship where we need to bring more definition to it so that we may move forward with it. When a boy meets a girl, it is appropriate to date, go for coffee, or take a walk as they get to know each other. If after five years, the same boy and girl are at the same stage in the relationship, there is probably something wrong, or it certainly has no future. Similarly, many relationships get stuck at the assumed stage and never move into a place of definition where we can begin to deepen the foundations of that relationship, making it "load-bearing" in our lives.

WHAT IS OUR PART IN DEVELOPING THESE RELATIONSHIPS?

For these relationships to become all that God has planned for them to be, it is important that we learn to sow into these relationships. There are many relationships God will bring us into that seem to have little relevance to our lives at this season. God, in His wisdom, knows that these relationships will become important or necessary at a later stage of our life. If we do not spend the time investing in these relationships, then they will never reach the place of maturity required for the work that God will call them to in our future.

A key principle is to pray and ask God for wisdom about these relationships.

All relationships exist within a context. Sometimes we need the wisdom to create a context around which a relationship can develop and become all that God wants it to be. If we do not use the wisdom to create those contexts, then usually the development will not take place.

It can also be important to understand that there are different levels of reciprocity in relationships. For example, there are mentoring relationships where somebody else is clearly speaking into our life, and we are in the position of the mentee, the person who is receiving guidance and instruction. There are other times in relationships when we are the ones in the mentoring role and are speaking into the lives of somebody else; there are also relationships where there is an equal level of reciprocity in the context of that relationship. If we do not take the time to think through what is actually going on in a relationship, we can often not allow God to do what he wishes to through that relationship. For any mentoring relationship to work, there needs to be a defined acknowledgment of what is actually happening in that relationship and the permission given for the person to speak into somebody's life. As a pastor of a local church, I will have many friends within the context of that church, but when somebody is coming to see me, I want to be clear if I am wearing my hat as the pastor, with permission to speak into the life, or are we simply two friends having lunch together?

RELATIONAL CONFLICT AND RESOLUTION

* * *

Every human relationship (that exists at any depth) will experience tension and conflict at times. It is theoretically possible to go through life with a collection of shallow and superficial relationships that avoid most situations of conflict. The problem with that scenario is the depth and connection in human relationships, which brings all of the treasure and beauty to those relationships.

How can we learn to deal with relational conflict and bring it to resolution?

The Bible says we should arm ourselves with the thought of suffering. (1 Peter 4:1, NKJV).

Firstly, while it can seem negative, there is power in being clear that conflict will happen. If we are engaged in a relationship and we are then surprised when there is misunderstanding, miscommunication, and an offense, we are not well positioned to resolve that conflict. When we know, as a certain fact, that conflict will come, we can arrange in advance how we will respond to that conflict. It is important that we recognize that when we are in conflict or offense, we all tend to make poor decisions. We have a tendency to look upon that conflict through the lens of a wounded heart. If we can decide in advance what our response will be to the certainty of conflict, then we posture ourselves to make good decisions.

"For now we see in a mirror, dimly, but then face to face. Now I know in part, but then I shall know just as I also am known." (1 Corinthians 13:12, NKJV).

* * *

A second step in conflict resolution is understanding that we all walk with broken and limited capacity to understand, communicate, and perceive things. Ninety five percent of relational conflict can come down to communication, perception, and expectations. The trouble lies in the fact that from our own perspective, we know our heart's motivation, we know what we think are the facts concerning a situation. We often feel, usually mistakenly, that we have communicated well to the other person, and we cannot understand how they can see the same situation in a completely different way. I think it is a really helpful thing to understand that all of us communicate poorly. To add to this truth, most of us tend to think of ourselves as somebody who communicates quite well. I've rarely found an exception to this rule. The challenge is it is actually hard to even know our own hearts.

"The heart is deceitful above all things, And desperately wicked; Who can know it?" (Jeremiah 17:9, NKJV).

It is hard to know our own hearts, it is doubly hard to effectively communicate with somebody else. Most of the time when we are communicating, we are only usually conveying around 20% of what we actually think and feel. A good rule of thumb regarding communication is that we should try to communicate five times more than we think we need to. We should then develop the habit of asking the other person what they have actually understood from our communication and seeing if they are able to then return that back to us.

Another great principle in terms of relational communication is the further we are removed from being in the same room with a person, the poorer communication will be. For many years, I have had a rule in ministry, both for myself and for others, that I never communicate anything important via a text message, email, or social media, etc. I will frequently use those methods of communication, but I use them to set up meetings, to communicate small, unimportant messages.

"Can we get together at 5 PM? Where shall we meet? Would you like coffee?"

The fallacy of most electronic communication is that when we, the writer communicate, we know what we are feeling, it makes sense to us, and we are wrapped up in our own dialogue. The person reading our text message is void of any human contact, any facial expression, vocal intonation or expression of the heart.

THE KEY OF HUMILITY

One of the greatest keys in helping resolve conflict, and indeed, avoiding conflict, is found in humility. The Bible states that God gives grace to the humble. (James 4:6, NKJV) When we approach relationships through the lens of humility, we are taking the lower road and allowing the other person the privilege of taking the high ground (Please add the Bible verse here). One of the greatest lessons I have ever learned in marriage counseling was the following: when two people are arguing, by definition they both think that they are right and that the other person is wrong. They are both eating from the tree of the knowledge of good and evil (Please add the Bible verse here). In fact, they are in a battle, albeit a verbal one, that basically says, "I am right and you are wrong." Whenever one of them will humble themselves and say, "I give you the right to win this battle," whenever somebody is willing to take the wrong upon themselves through humility, then grace is released to the other person. There is a powerful lesson we can all learn that the tree of life is greater than the tree of knowledge of good or evil. What is important in any relationship, whether marriage, friendship, kingdom relationship, etc., is not actually about who is right. The key question is who is inviting the grace of God into that relationship.

"Confess your trespasses to one another, and pray for one another, that you may be healed. The effective, fervent prayer of a righteous man avails much." (James 5:16, NKJV).

Like many others before me, I have found that when I lower my defenses, humble myself, and give the other person the win, God will quickly turn the hearts around, and they in turn will begin to see things from my perspective. Either way, the key is not about winning the argument, but about winning the relationship. If we can learn the simple, and yet powerful, lesson of separating out the relationship from the conflict, it becomes easy to resolve things. The danger, for all of us, in relational conflict is, we tend to lock our identity into our argument. We also make the mistake of attaching the other person's identity to their point of view. It is actually very easy to say to somebody, "I love you, and this relationship is of infinite value to me. We obviously see some things differently and possibly we may never agree, but I refuse to devalue you and let go of this relationship." If we will fight for the relationship, rather than fighting for the argument to be won, we will usually win both the former and often the latter.

Another key to relational conflict is simply tabling the

discussion. I have learned after much difficult experience that if I am in a conflictual situation with somebody, I will often tell them how much I love and value them and ask them if we can come back in several days and talk some more about our disagreement. By emphasizing our love, and the value to our lives, and pushing the discussion back several days, we are often giving the Holy Spirit a chance to work in our own hearts, and indeed the heart of the other person. My experience usually when we come back to that discussion is that things are a lot easier; we are approaching the subject with an attitude of grace and humility. Our emotions become inflamed quickly, but it is actually quite difficult to maintain that intensity of feeling for a few days.

LEARNING TO FORGIVE

One of the most important lessons we can ever learn in the Christian life is that of how to forgive others. Jesus said it is impossible that the offenses do not come (Luke 17:1, NKJV). Every one of us, at times, will walk through seasons where we need to forgive others. Forgiving others is actually a very simple process, but it is one that confuses many people. When we find ourselves in a situation where we feel that we have been wronged or treated poorly by others, it is so easy for our emotions to engage and begin to dictate the state of our heart. The key to forgiveness is simply understanding that forgiveness is a choice of our will not a feeling, or emotion that we experience. When we need to forgive somebody, we can choose to do so as an act of our volition or free will, and then we need to forgive by faith, and not by feeling. If we will hold a position by faith in our hearts that a certain person is forgiven, then sooner or later, our emotions will come back into line with the declared position of our will. If we allow ourselves the luxury of evaluating that situation through the lens of what was done or said about us, etc., then we will arrive at a place of unforgiveness. It is possible to forgive somebody even if they will never admit they were wrong. It is possible to forgive somebody even if they are no longer alive on the Earth. Forgiveness actually has nothing to do with the other person, and everything to do with our own hearts before the Lord. Jesus is crystal clear that if we will not forgive others for the trespasses against us, neither will our Heavenly Father forgive us. Sobering, but true words. Unforgiveness is like drinking poison and expecting the other person to die.

LEARNING TO LOOK AT RELATIONSHIPS FROM GOD'S PERSPECTIVE.

In the past few years, many of us have heard a lot of teaching on the subject of our identity in Christ. This is a wonderful and foundational truth of the Christian life. We have learned not to look at ourselves through the eyes of our natural identity but to allow the word of God to define who we really are. While this truth is a glorious and amazing one, most of us have only heard the truth applied to ourselves. We have looked at these teachings and applied them to our own personal lives but all too often have not applied them to our brothers and sisters around us. While it is important and vital that we understand that we are in Christ, it is equally important that we learn to see others through that identity as well. God does not call us to build kingdom relationships. Rather, God has called us into a family and is teaching us to learn to "know no man after the flesh" (2 Corinthians 5:16, NKJV). We need to learn to know one another after the spirit.

So often in church circles, we have seen the inefficiencies in one another and felt that it was our mission to call somebody out on the faults and failings. I believe that in our relationship, rather than calling somebody out on their behavior, God wants us to call somebody up to their identity. Our job is to stand in the gap. Our role is to fill the gap between where somebody actually is at this current time and who heaven has called them to be. Our role is to cheer them on as they journey. Instead of condemning somebody for who they are and casting the first stone (Please add the Bible verse here), our call and mission is to prophetically encourage them while it is yet and remind them constantly who God says they are.

The local church should be the place where the greatest relationships on planet Earth exist. God does not call us to a local church because we agree with everybody, on everything. God does not call us to a local church because we can naturally relate to everybody. The local church is the greatest test for a Christian. The question is not do we naturally gravitate to the people assembled in a church, but rather can we learn to love them through the love of Christ. There is a wonderful point in the life of believers when we realize our own inability to love others as God would have us do so. It is only at that point that we begin to draw upon the grace of God to build kingdom relationships.

Take some time to write out a vision for the

relationships in your life. Take inventory of the current relationships that you have. Learn to come to God and ask him questions about your family and friends.

How does he see them? Who are you called to be to them?
Who are they called to be to you?
Which are the relationships that God wants you to put much

focus on in this season?

Are there relationships he wants you to back away from in this season?

Are the new relationships he wishes to bring into your life in this season?

Take some time to look over the following questions and write out your own personal vision statement for this area of your life.

Questions for Meditation

- *Are there ideas and scripts about this area of your life that heaven wants to rewrite in this season?*

- *What are the challenges you have in relation to this subject? Describe them as past, defeated, and nailed to the cross.*

- *What is the Lord displacing in your life? What new thing does He want to replace the old with?*

- *How does God define my identity?*

- *Describe the relationship that God is calling you to have with Him in this area.*

- *If God were saying "Yes and Amen", what would your request be?*

- *What would living in complete freedom, joy, and victory look like?*

- *What promise is God speaking over you in this season? What are the promises He is calling you to declare back to Him?*

- *What would transformation look like under your present circumstances?*

- *What would it take for you to develop a mindset, a lifestyle, a persona of fullness as a way of life?*

- *How are you called to minister to others?*

Chapter Eleven

Hearing God's Voice

Christianity is a journey, and God calls us to walk with Him along the way (Psalm 32:8). If we simply consider our Christian life as adhering to a set of beliefs, we miss out on its essence. As followers of Jesus, we are on a journey, but we are not alone; we walk with a guide within us. We are learning to live by inside information. It is crucial that we learn to allow the Holy Spirit to lead and guide us on this journey.

In this chapter, we will explore together how to develop a vision for hearing from God and receiving guidance from Him. The information contained in this chapter is vital and often lacking in many churches. I invite you to allow the Holy Spirit to expand the boundaries of your faith in this area as you read the words of this chapter. (John 10:27) I believe that the Lord wants to invite you to elevate your walk with Him and your relationship with Him as someone who can clearly and accurately speak into your life.

I cherish hearing from God. I love it when God speaks in a clear way that nobody can deny. I revel in moments when God reveals things to me that nobody else could know and uses that knowledge to manifest His glory and grace. God is a communicator, a living God who delights in sharing with His children. Many years ago, during a ministry trip to India, I passed by a store selling idols. Perhaps due to my inquisitive nature, I decided to step inside and converse with the owner. Upon entering, the owner warmly greeted me, likely mistaking me for a Western tourist with money to spend. He proudly displayed his collection of idols and deities on the shelves. As I browsed, I inquired if he had a god who could speak.

The owner looked at me strangely and simply replied, "A God who speaks? Who ever heard of such a thing?" "Indeed," I responded. I then asked if he had a god who could embrace my children. Regrettably, the answer was a polite no. Lastly, I explained that I was a sinner from a long line of sinners and wondered if he had any gods capable of forgiving sins. Sadly, they were also out of stock that day.

"Whoever heard of a God who speaks?"

In this chapter, we will cover principles of how we can learn to hear God's voice clearly and accurately. We will discuss potential pitfalls and how to avoid them, with the promise of a life built upon the leading and guidance of the Holy Spirit. In our quest to develop a personal vision, it is crucial that we refrain from relying solely on our own understanding and instead allow the Lord to direct us in all our endeavors. (Proverbs 3:56) God has a magnificent plan for our lives, and the Holy Spirit has been sent to lead and guide us into that plan. (John 16:13)

One of the most dramatic transformations that can take place in our life is when we begin to learn to hear from God. My own journey with this began in the mid1980s. I came to know the Lord Jesus through a Billy Graham Crusade in Liverpool, England, in July 1984. I joined a good local church and began growing in the things of God, and from a very early stage of my Christian development felt the call of God upon my life to step into full-time ministry. The church I was part of was a Spiritfilled church (a Pentecostal church); we believed in the supernatural, in prophecy, and in a God who wanted to intervene in our lives. In spite of this, these things always seemed to function at a low level of general encouragement and exhortation. To be clear, there is absolutely nothing wrong with this, and it can be a beautiful and valid thing. It was only after about four years of my growth that I began to see people move in a realm that was much more accurate and specific. I spent some time working with an evangelist who moved really clearly in the word of knowledge ministry. Again and again, the Lord would give this man specific conditions, parts of the body that needed healing, people's names, where they were located in the room, etc. What moved me the most was not actually the ability to hear from God in terms of ministry to others. I was greatly impacted when I realized that God wanted to speak to each of us personally. That he would show us things that would happen during our day. That he wanted to walk and talk with us in the intimate details of our life. He wanted to share his heart and love for us.

Over the years, I have noticed many people's grid for understanding the subject of hearing from God is only framed in a ministry setting, upon a stage. I have no problem with that per se, and usually move in those things myself on a regular basis. In spite of that, my greatest joy is to hear from God, to walk with him, and talk with him. There is something glorious and transformational that takes place in our lives when we no longer have a long distance relationship with God. I truly believe most people never really hear from God from year to year. Many of these people live with a vague sense that they may be out of the will of God. They know in a general biblical sense that God loves them, but they never actually spend time with him in a two way relationship that involves communication.

I have discovered that one of the greatest tools in sharing our faith with others can be to hear from God. We live in a culture where most people have a natural resistance to believing that God is actually real. There are many people for whom, at least here in America, if somebody approaches them and attempts to share the truth of the gospel, their eyes will glaze over, defenses come up, and they close their hearts to hearing any truth. Hearing from God is not the only way we can break through that wall of protection, but I believe it is one of the most powerful and effective. When God is able to show us something about a person that we could not possibly have known, then the reality of God's existence, and indeed, His interest in that person, breaks into their life in a way that is often dramatic and life changing.

Around 20 years ago while based in France, I was on a ministry tour visiting churches in the United States. One day, while ministering at a church in New England I decided to visit a local supermarket. As I was walking around the supermarket, I began praying in my heart and said, "Lord, I would love to speak to somebody here, please lead and direct me to someone." I went around the supermarket for about 10 minutes, and the place seemed completely deserted. I could not find anybody to talk to, and I didn't feel any leading from God. In the end, I went to the only checkout that was staffed and open, and there was a long queue of people waiting at it. I have to confess, patience is not my strongest spiritual gift, and I began internally complaining to God about waiting at this checkout queue.

When I eventually got to the head of the queue, a young lady began scanning my groceries. While doing so, she turned to me with a smile on her face and said, "How is your day going?" Without thinking, I heard myself say, "How is your adultery going?" Jesus said, "Take no thought in that day what you will say, for it is not you who speak, but the Spirit of your Father who speaks in you" (Matthew 10:20).

The young lady behind the checkout was visibly shocked and terrified. I went on to prophesy to her and said that she was a Christian, she had been brought up in the things of God, but was now involved in a relationship with a married man. I prophesied to her and said, God's word to her was "grace, grace, grace." God was not condemning her, but he was inviting her to come back to him because he loved her. I got to briefly pray with this girl before leaving.

I want you to see a really important key from this incident. The dramatic word that impacted the girl was not the word that told her she was having an adulterous affair. She knew she was having an affair. She did not need a Christian to tell her that. The dramatic word was simply, "God loves you and is calling you back to himself." That is the thing she did not know. That is the thing she needed to hear. What I want you to see is that she probably would not have paid much attention to the latter message without the former one. That one word, "adultery," was enough to demonstrate to her the reality of God and the weight and truthfulness of the second word.

* * *

God has things to say to every person in this world. God has keys that will unlock the hardest heart and the most resistant person. He is not interested in speaking to us to make us look good or to impress others. Everything God does works from a place of love that he may reveal his grace, compassion, and mercy to this dying world.

The purpose of this chapter is an invitation to dream. I want to invite you to use your sanctified imagination and to dream what life would look like if you were constantly in communication with God. What would life look like if you were sharing your heart with God every day, and He was sharing His heart with you? What would life look like if each and every day God was speaking to you about His love for you, about the things that would happen to you that day, about your relationships, about every aspect of your life and walk with Him? This is the life God invites us to. This is the only Christian life the Bible describes.

Those who are the sons of God are those who are led by the Spirit of God (Romans 8:14).

Learning to hear from God is much less about technique, formula, and methodology. It has everything to do with relationship. The key to knowing God's voice is knowing God's heart. The key to being led by the Spirit is found in sonship with God.

I once had a supernatural experience, which really imprinted this concept onto my heart. I think it is the only time I have heard the audible voice of God in my life. I was teaching one day in a

Bible school in Paris, France, about the topic of finding God's will and calling for our life. As I taught I made the statement: "Prophetic revelation, reveals the will of God," suddenly, I heard the voice of God shout "No". The Lord spoke to my heart. He said "it is possible to know the will of God, and completely miss the heart of God. He continued to say, "But anybody who connects with the heart of God, will always end up in the will of God."

Can it be dangerous to try to hear God's voice for ourselves? My answer would be emphatically, yes, it can be dangerous. If we've been around the Christian world for any amount of time, particularly in charismatic circles, we will have seen examples of people who have created all kinds of foolishness when they thought they were hearing from God. I have seen people make terrible mistakes in life through this subject. I have often seen Christians try to tell other people what is God's will for their life and cause havoc and destruction in this way. In recent years here in America, we have seen the body of Christ come into disrepute when internet prophets have tried to prophesy who will win elections. I would completely empathize and understand anybody who would look at the subject and feel it was dangerous and want to avoid it. I have known many pastors of local churches who simply come to the conclusion that life is a lot easier and cleaner if people simply follow the Bible and never really try to hear from God themselves.

I agree it is completely true that life is safer in that manner. I do not agree that this is biblical. God does not want us to throw the baby out with the bathwater. The answer to a poor example of somebody trying to hear from God is a right example of somebody hearing from God.

* * *

I believe there are steps we can take to keep us safe from falling into error on this subject, both in our individual life and in the lives of the wider church.

The first thing that will protect us in this arena of hearing from God is always placing the Bible, God's written word, above any individual leading or sense of God speaking to us. Whenever we attempt to hear from God, we must test that by God's word. The Bible, God's word, comes pretested. (2 Timothy 3:1617) God's word is the final authority over everything in our lives.

The second step to avoiding the pitfalls of trying to hear from God is the key of humility. Whenever we enter a situation and believe that we are greater than anybody else, that we have our own personal hotline to God that others do not have, we are in danger of falling. God gives grace to the humble (James 4:6). Humility is such a protector. When we are humble, we will not mind apologizing when we get things wrong. We know in part, we see in part, we see through a glass darkly (1 Corinthians 13:12). This verse is in the context of prophecy and hearing from God. I have noticed that those who try to be dramatic when talking about hearing from God are often those who hear very little. The people who stand up and boldly proclaim, "Thus says the Lord!" rarely have anything of revelation to say. The people who actually walk closely with God and really hear His voice will often be heard saying things like, "I could be wrong here, but I think God might be saying this." We make up in entertainment what we lack in power.

Another step that will protect us in hearing from God is walking in a committed expression of a local church community.

Nothing is more dangerous than being a lone ranger. We all need each other. God will never give one person all of the revelation they need. We all need the security of having other people discern whether we truly are hearing from God or whether we are simply following our own hearts.

"Let one person speak and let the other judge" (1 Corinthians 14:29).

It is important when we are hearing from God to realize that there are three vital steps, and if we confuse these, we can get ourselves into trouble and cause problems.

1. Revelation.
2. Interpretation.
3. Application.

Revelation is the process of us hearing from God, of God revealing something to our human spirit (which is connected to the spirit of Christ, 1 Corinthians 6:17). Revelation comes entirely from God.

Interpretation is our understanding of how to understand what God has revealed, what this actually means in any given circumstance or situation. It is possible to receive a correct revelation from God, but to add our own interpretation to that revelation. Joseph correctly heard from God in his dreams, but he interpreted that his brothers would serve him, rather than understanding that he would serve his brothers. (Genesis 37:511)

Application is the process of understanding how we apply this revelation and interpretation in a practical sense in our life or in the lives of others. Without the step of application, revelation will only inflate our egos and heads.

When the Holy Spirit moved on the day of Pentecost, the correct response of the people was, "What does this signify, and what should we now do in response?" (Acts 2:12)

In all of these three steps, we must be dependent on God, be a people who walk in the Word, and rely on the community of our brothers and sisters (the local church).

Around 20 years ago, I was leading a church congregation in France, and I was also traveling internationally in itinerant ministry. France is a very difficult nation to preach the gospel in, and there is much persecution that goes on from the government against local church communities. Any Bible believing or evangelical church would be viewed in France as a cult or a sect and come under frequent scrutiny from the government. There was a time in 2005 when I was ministering in the United States and staying with the pastor and his family in Massachusetts. One night, while staying in this pastor's home, I had a vivid dream about the FBI bursting into this pastor's home and searching the house from top to bottom. In my dream, the FBI found nothing amiss and then apologized to the family and left. In the morning, I went to my pastor friend, and I told him I had had a dream about him, and that he was going to be investigated by the American authorities. This was not exactly an edifying or encouraging word to receive first thing in the morning before breakfast! I went away, feeling proud of myself that I could hear from God so accurately.

Two days later, the French Minister of the Interior

department burst into my church in France in the middle of a Wednesday evening service and demanded to see all of our paperwork, the IDs of everybody present. They searched our church premises from top to bottom, and eventually, when they found nothing amiss, they left. My revelation had been completely accurate, my interpretation was completely inaccurate, and my application was useless. I wish that when I had had the initial dream, I had gone back to the Lord and inquired of Him about what this meant, and how I should react to it. I wish that when the French authorities had burst into my church, we would have been live streaming the event, we would have baked brownies with "Welcome French authorities" written on them. "However, when He, the Spirit of truth, has come, He will guide you into all truth" (John 16:13).

Let us examine some practical steps that will help us in learning to hear God's voice and walking in the guidance of the Holy Spirit.

RELATIONSHIP

The most foundational truth I know in terms of hearing from God is all about relationship. God does not want us to learn techniques, formulas, or methods to hear from him. The primary truth of hearing from God is simply this: We will hear from God to the depth of our relationship with him. Any knowledge or technique we think we know will fail if we walk in a shallow relationship with him. The most common problems in relation to hearing from God are simply this: Am I hearing from God? Am I hearing from myself? Am I hearing from Satan? Resolution to this problem is found in the secret place and digging the wells of relationship with God.

* * *

Learn to spend time every day in quietness, personal worship, and intimacy before the Lord. When we are hearing from God in small, frequent ways every day, we will begin to hear from him in the larger things of life.

FAITH

Faith is such a wonderful key to hearing from God. It took me a long time to realize this. God speaks to faith. Satan speaks to fear. Many times God will speak to us, but if we do not believe it is God speaking to us, that will quench the Holy Spirit, and he will no longer speak. In 1 Samuel 3, God speaks to Samuel as a young boy, yet Samuel does not believe he is hearing from God. God does not continue to speak to Samuel because Samuel does not believe it is God speaking. It is only when Samuel acknowledges that this is actually God speaking that God continues the conversation. ("Speak, Lord, for your servant hears." 1 Samuel 3:9)

We need to begin to develop a simple and consistent faith that we can hear from God. "My sheep hear My voice." (John 10:27) Every day you can consistently declare, on the basis of God's word alone, that you do hear from God. When we hear from God in small ways every day and take the time to acknowledge that it is indeed him speaking to us, then we will grow in that confidence.

RISK

John Wimber used to say, "Faith is spelled R.I.S.K."

* * *

184

From heaven's point of view, God speaking (God's word) is a certainty. God is the most sure thing in the universe (2 Peter 1). There is another reality from our point of view, in our flesh, that when we try to hear from God, we will always be taking a risk. Every time we move in the spirit, a chasm of fear will open up before us, the fear of making a mistake or getting it wrong will present itself before us. There are many practical ways of dealing with this. I believe if we are to be a people who consistently hear from God, we must embrace a lifestyle of risk. The Archbishop of Canterbury once said, "the church should be a safe place to take crazy risks."

GROWING IN THIS AREA

One of the most important stages in the development of a young baby is learning to hear the voice of its parents. Normally speaking, a child will not learn to hear and speak a language at a school. Rather, they will sit on the lap of the parents and play, listen, and imitate. A child does not listen to the voice of its parents with the dictionary in hand and try to intellectually understand what this means. Rather, they hear the heart of the parent being expressed over time. They add significance and meaning to the specific words spoken. The challenge in the body of Christ is trying to learn to hear from God in a prophetic conference or reading a book. We need to learn to be little children again. Children have permission to get things wrong. When a child learns to walk, it will usually take a step or two and fall on its nose and cry. We do not consider this a mistake; rather, we take a video and share it with our friends. Every Christian should learn to hear from God by taking baby steps and not think it strange when we make mistakes. We do not need to hide or justify them but realize they are a natural part of our growth process in God.

ACCOUNTABILITY

When it comes to hearing from God, it is vital that we are actually hearing from Him and not simply deceiving ourselves or indeed others. Hearing from God is one of the areas in the Christian life that it is actually very possible to test and demonstrate. I believe it is important that everybody moving in this realm is open to accountability. It functions on two levels: the first is personal accountability. It is important that we are honest with ourselves. When we believe we have heard from God, it is good that we put that to the test. Obviously, we want to test whether what we are hearing is biblical, in line with sound biblical doctrine, and consistent with the heart of God. But we also want to verify whether what we hear from God is actually correct. If God shows us that somebody has a certain condition, do they actually have that condition? If God shows us that something will come to pass, did it actually come to pass? The charismatic world is full of Christians who live in a mishmash of fuzzy "words from God" that do not really say anything. I believe we should set the bar high and believe for accurate specific things that will bring God glory and advance the kingdom of God on the Earth.

Everybody endeavoring to hear from God should also be open to accountability from others. The primary, and the best way, that this functions is within the context of a local church. The local church should be a community of people on a journey of learning to hear from God. Within that context, we should be able to test words both to see that they align with the Bible and also that they come to pass.

* * *

PRACTICAL WAYS THAT GOD SPEAKS

There are many practical ways in which God speaks. They are too numerous to list. God can speak through a myriad of different ways to his people. In a very real sense, the issue is not how God speaks but whether our hearts are in a place of receptivity to hear from him.

Here are some of the practical ways I have found that God will speak. We should not be limited to this list and should learn to recognize different ways. God will speak to us personally:

The still small voice in your mind. Take a moment, and count to 10 in your mind right now. That is often how you will pick up.

Vision. I have had several times in my life when God has given me an open vision, something I could see as real as the world around me. I have had thousands of times when God has given me a mental visual impression. This can be hard to see and be more subjective, but it is a frequent way that God speaks to us. In your mind right now, visualize a dog. You probably did not see the letters D.O.G fly past the screen of your mind. You probably had a visual impression or picture of a dog. This is a common way that God can speak to us.

A knowing in our hearts. Sometimes God can give us a certain knowing that does not make rational sense. We simply know something without understanding how that knowledge has come.

God can use our physical body to draw attention to something. When ministering in a meeting, this will happen to me frequently. I will feel a pain in my body or pressure; it is simply God wanting to draw my attention to the fact that there is someone present with that condition. When I pray for that person, the pain will go away.

While there are many ways that God can speak, the key is simply this: come back to the witness of the Holy Spirit in your heart. The same witness that tells you that you are a child of God is the same witness that will say, "this is my voice" in your heart. As we practice this, we move away from subjectivity into a greater place of relational certainty.

"You will hear a voice behind you saying, 'This is the way, walk in it,' whenever you turn to the right or to the left." (Isaiah 30:21)

BUILDING HISTORY

As we continue to hear from God, and we learn to differentiate between our own voice and the voice of God, we will begin to build a personal history in this area. Hearing from God is not something we could learn in a school or college, only through practical and relational experience. The more we build this personal history and confidence, the more we will grow in this area. It is also a place where, as we build personal history, other people will begin to notice and respect our ability in this area. It is important that we do not demand this respect from others but rather that we earn it through the history that we have built.

"So Samuel grew, and the Lord was with him and let none of

his words fall to the ground. And all Israel from Dan to Beersheba knew that Samuel had been established as a prophet of the Lord. Then the Lord appeared again in Shiloh. For the Lord revealed Himself to Samuel in Shiloh by the word of the Lord." (1 Samuel 3:1921)

WALKING THIS OUT IN COMMUNITY

We should all be part of a local church community that is committed to hearing God's voice together. It is not sufficient that a church believes in these things as a doctrinal position; it must also teach, instruct, and create a practical place for the Holy Spirit to speak. Any church that does not teach and make a place for the gifts of the Holy Spirit to flow in their gatherings is simply not following the clear teaching of scripture. We can determine what we truly believe by what we consistently do. I believe in committed financial giving and hence I make a regular place for an offering in all church services.

As a church makes a place for people to hear from God and move in the gifts, they must also have protocols for this to be done in order, and to oversee this in a godly manner. I will allow all my church members to prophesy in public, but I also ask that they join a team where we have a context to train and give feedback to those who want this freedom.

God has marvelous things to say and declare to you. You will never be a complete child of your father until you can hear His voice. Begin this journey today.

Take some time to write down a vision of how you want to

live your life, in terms of hearing from God, the guidance and leading of the Holy Spirit, and God, using you to share his heart with others. Take some time to ponder over these questions.

Questions for Meditation

- *Are there ideas and scripts about this area of your life that heaven wants to rewrite in this season?*

- *What are the challenges you have in relation to this subject? Describe them as past, defeated, and nailed to the cross.*

- *What is the Lord displacing in your life? What new thing does He want to replace the old with?*

- *How does God define my identity?*

- *Describe the relationship that God is calling you to have with Him in this area.*

- *If God were saying "Yes and Amen", what would your request be?*

- *What would living in complete freedom, joy, and victory look like?*

- *What promise is God speaking over you in this season? What are the promises He is calling you to declare back to Him?*

- *What would transformation look like under your present circumstances?*

- *What would it take for you to develop a mindset, a lifestyle, a persona of fullness as a way of life?*

- *How are you called to minister to others?*

Chapter Twelve

The Disciplines of the Kingdom

In this chapter, we will explore the essence of a disciplined christian life. This encompasses not just a relationship with God, and faith in His Word but also our responses and actions reflecting those beliefs. If our Christian life revolves solely around a set of beliefs and doctrines, it does not genuinely reflect the essence of Christianity.

James, the apostle, addresses this crucial issue in his epistle, highlighting the incongruity of claiming faith without corresponding actions. James 2:17 states, "Thus also faith by itself, if it does not have works, is dead." The term "works" here implies actions that align with faith. While we affirm salvation by Grace alone and our faith in the finished works of Jesus, it is essential to recognize that our faith, if genuine, inevitably translates into tangible actions. Encountering the transformative power of Jesus should profoundly impact our daily lives and how we practically live.

Spiritual disciplines serve as avenues of Grace, enabling us to deepen our spiritual journey by incorporating specific Christian practices into our daily routines. These practices intricately weave the truths of heaven into the fabric of our lives, enriching our walk with the Savior. We aim to explore these spiritual disciplines together, offering insights into ten practices (among many others) that can nurture and fortify your Christian faith as you journey with the Savior, drawing from the wisdom of the Bible.

John 8:3136 (NKJV)

31 Then Jesus said to those Jews who believed Him, "If you abide in My word, you are My disciples indeed. 32 And you shall know the truth, and the truth shall make you free."

33 They answered Him, "We are Abraham's descendants, and have never been in bondage to anyone. How can You say, 'You will be made free'?"

34 Jesus answered them, "Most assuredly, I say to you, whoever commits sin is a slave of sin. 35 And a slave does not abide in the house forever, but a son abides forever. 36 Therefore if the Son makes you free, you shall be free indeed.

One of the greatest challenges for many Christians is discerning if they are truly born again; they may love God, yet their spiritual life seems overshadowed by life's demands. Many struggle to maintain a vital connection with God, feeling overwhelmed by worldly influences. Simply attending a church on Sundays often feels like the only lifeline keeping them spiritually afloat. This frustration is shared by many, and finding a solution can seem daunting. We are all creatures of habit. To sustain and thrive in our Christian faith, we must cultivate heavenly habits here on Earth. In John's gospel, Jesus emphasizes that His disciples are those who continue in His word. (John 8:31) What does it truly mean to embody the habit of continuing in the Word?

When we create a habit, we automate a process in our life. When we create a habit, at least to some degree, we bypass our willpower and take away a measure of our choice and streamline decision making processes. This is obviously a bad thing when we are talking about unhealthy or bad habits, but the same internal mechanism can be a powerful tool when applied in a good direction. We have a tendency to look at Christianity as something we acquire, like becoming a member of a club. We say a prayer and ask Jesus to come into our hearts, and then consider ourselves as members of his family. This is true, but not the truth, is true, but shallow.

We are called to be followers of Jesus. Disciples who are practicing this new life. As we practice the new habits of the kingdom of God, we embed the life of Jesus into the fabric of our everyday lives. I am a guitar player. As with all good musicians, I practice. I have played for many years, but I have regular times when I will sit down with a guitar, and a metronome, and practice both existing skills and work upon new ones. If we are truly followers of Jesus, we need to practice the word of God in our daily lives.

Our identity in Christ, and everything we have as children of God, comes to us through the finished work of Jesus. In heavenly places, we have everything we need. We are full, we are free, we are glorious. When we practice spiritual disciplines, we engage in the action of bringing the realities of heaven down into our lives upon the earth. It is not enough that we simply acknowledge that these things are true in heaven. God wants us to practice heaven's life here on Earth until that becomes a normal part of our daily life. Jesus taught us to pray that God's kingdom would come, God's will would be done on earth as it is in heaven. (Matthew 6:10) When we practice spiritual disciplines, we are practicing bringing heaven into our daily lives.

Matthew 11:2830 MSG
"Are you tired? Worn out? Burned out on religion? Come to me. Get away with me and you'll recover your life. I'll show you how to take a real rest. Walk with me and work with me—watch how I do it. Learn the unforced rhythms of grace. I won't lay anything heavy or ill fitting on you. Keep company with me and you'll learn to live freely and lightly."

Spiritual disciplines are the places where we learn the unforced rhythms of grace. We are not earning anything through spiritual disciplines, but rather, we are practicing the life that we already possess in Christ Jesus. Spiritual disciplines become a meeting place and an access point to the grace of God that is already available to us. "Through Him, we have also obtained access by faith into this grace in which we stand, and we rejoice in hope of the glory of God." Romans 5:2

God's grace is freely available to every believer, but not every believer walks in the same portion of that grace in life. We need to train our hearts in grace. "But grow in the grace and knowledge of our Lord and Savior Jesus Christ." 2 Peter 3:18. We need to practice accessing the grace of God by faith and bringing it into our daily lives.

When discussing Christian disciplines, it is vital that we

understand what they are not. It can be easy for Christians to view disciplines as a means to earn something from God. Rather, the foundational truth is to realize that we have already received everything from God, but we are practicing that which we have already received. "Therefore, my beloved, as you have always obeyed, not as in my presence only, but now much more in my absence, work out your own salvation with fear and trembling; for it is God who works in you both to will and to do for His good pleasure." Philippians 2:1213

When practicing spiritual disciplines, we are working out our salvation, not working for our salvation. (Philippians 2:12) God has already completed all the works on the cross of Calvary. (John 19:30) As we work out our salvation, God is working in us. We work out; God works in.

The letter to the Galatians is based upon this foundational truth. Paul is literally furious with the people of Galatia, who have turned aside from the grace of God and have gone back to the Jewish law to try to earn the standing and status as the righteous people of God. (Galatians 1:6) Paul asserts that there is nothing they can do to earn the grace of God. God's grace is simply that: it is grace, unmerited, undeserved, and unearned favor. When we speak about spiritual disciplines, it is helpful to realize that before we ever do anything, we have already received all we, need because of Jesus. (Ephesians 2:89)

It would be preferable for a Christian not to engage in some spiritual disciplines if they are simply done as a means of religious observance, and a replacement strategy for the blood of Jesus.

* * *

Take, for example, the biblical concept of fasting. Fasting is a powerful tool; it is something that Jesus commanded all believers to do. And yet, it is easy for immature believers to look at fasting as a means to earn something from God. I have a Christian friend who wanted to receive healing from God. This man decided he was going to fast until God healed him. After 10 days of fasting, the Lord spoke to him and told him to "arise and eat." When he replied, "Lord, I am fasting," the Lord said, "No, you were not; you were on a hunger strike." Fasting is a powerful tool, but the key is to realize that fasting does not change God; fasting changes us. Fasting does not get God in a good mood to give something. We do not earn brownie points with God through fasting. Rather, fasting is a tool to change ourselves. Fasting is a means to posture our hearts, to break the power of unbelief, to refocus our souls, so that we may receive what God has already freely given. "And of His fullness we have all received, grace for grace." John 1:16

A good and legitimate question would be to ask how we can tell the difference between genuine spiritual discipline and dead works. There is a thin line between these two, and it can honestly be hard to differentiate at times in our life. I believe that the answer to that question is found in the secret place. The answer is found in the grace of God. The answer to that question is found in a relationship with God. When attempting to differentiate between a dead work and a spiritual discipline that will bring life into our being, it can be good to ask some of the following questions:

- Do I believe God will love me more when I do this thing?
- If I did not engage in this spiritual practice for a period

of time, how would it change my relationship with God?

- Do I feel any guilt or shame when I do not engage in this spiritual practice?
- Do I believe I will attain something at the end of this spiritual practice?

It is vital that we realize that God loves us, even if we never engage in any of these spiritual disciplines. I do not read my Bible so that God will love me. Rather, I know that God loves me, and hence I read my Bible. If you never give another dollar in your entire Christian walk to the cause of Christ, God loves you. God is not good to us because we are good; rather, God is good towards us because he is good. The key to not falling into the error of dead works all centers around the concept of identity. As we have said in a previous chapter, in the old covenant, God is judging our identity based upon performance. In Christ Jesus, we have been given our identity as a gift. Thus the things we do, the spiritual disciplines for example, are the natural outworking of that identity. We are working from, not working for. (Ephesians 2:89) Having received everything, we are walking out that life rather than trying to earn it.

In Christ Jesus, you are free, you are free indeed. "Therefore if the Son makes you free, you shall be free indeed." John 8:36. You are free to practice these things, and they are beneficial to you, but it is also vitally important to realize that you are free not to do these things. Paul says in Galatians 5:1, "Stand fast therefore in the liberty by which Christ has made us free." Another version says that it is for freedom that Christ has set us free. We are a free people. When we practice spiritual disciplines, we are learning to practice our freedoms. We are working them out, not working for them.

* * *

We are all creatures of habit. If you take the time to think about it, probably 99% of the things we do, or possibly a lot more, take place at an unconscious level.

Have you brushed your teeth today? Probably, the answer is yes. If I were to ask you why you have brushed your teeth today, what would your answer be? I am sure most of us could wax eloquent about the desire to have healthy teeth and gums, oral hygiene, the desire for beautiful, presentable teeth. While all of this is true, I am sure for the vast majority of us, none of these thoughts entered into our consciousness when, probably like myself this morning, you brushed your teeth. Why then did we complete this important task? There are really two primary answers. The main one is that from a very young age, we were trained and mentored by our parents to do so. We were not given the option of engaging in this habit, or not. After a period of time, we have embedded this habit into the fabric of our lives, we no longer think about it. Occasionally, when we are not able to brush our teeth, we probably feel uncomfortable, we feel what one might call the "gunk factor" in our lives. I do not brush my teeth for your sake; my parents are no longer alive here on the Earth (although very much so in heaven). I practice the disciplined habit of brushing my teeth for the joy and pleasure that it produces in my own life.

As we contemplate the practice of automating habits within our Christian walk, a pertinent question to pose is: what habits do we aspire to build into the fabric of our daily lives? It is true that many of us, as human beings, struggle with longterm planning. To some extent, most of us are living today with the cumulative choices we have made over the past several years. At times, we yearn for short term change, yet we are not always effective at implementing the ongoing small, micro changes necessary to achieve longterm goals. I would highly recommend the book "Atomic Habits" by James Clear. The premise of this book is that by altering small, micro, or atomic habits, we can gradually accumulate changes over time that will alter the course of our lives.

A good method of determining the habits we wish to work on is to reflect on the long range impact they will have on our lives. For instance, I encourage you to sit down and contemplate what, at the end of your life, you would look back on with gratitude. Our lives are filled with many habits, some of which we will undoubtedly regret later on. Many of them are simply innocuous, but others, like compound interest, will build over time and yield glorious results for us.

As we work together to formulate a personal vision of who we are and how we intend to live before God on this earth, it is a powerful exercise to delineate the overarching vision and then contemplate what habits such a person would possess. For instance, if we aspire to be individuals deeply rooted in the Bible, living by its principles and allowing it to shape our lives, it would be advantageous to inquire: What habits would characterize such a person, particularly in terms of daily Bible reading, study, and confession of the word. I encourage you to engage in this process to both cultivate an overarching vision of the person God is calling you to be and then to break down that longterm vision into daily practices.

It is also important to recognize that there are times and seasons in our lives when the Lord may desire to focus on a specific area of our lives. While it is essential for all of us to engage in certain foundational disciplines, we must allow the Holy Spirit to guide us and discern the season we are in. One remarkable aspect of God is that He never reacts to the past but is always present, and guiding us towards the future. The Holy Spirit always moves us towards where the "puck" is going, not where it currently is. We are in fellowship with the wisest person in the universe who knows both the future world, and what we need to become. It is one thing to envision what God has in store for us in the future; it is another to envision who we need to become to grow into that role.

God spoke to David about the day he would become king over Israel. (1 Samuel 16:1213) The role of king is one of authority and position that David would step into. While God was interested in David occupying this role and leading Israel, He was also interested in David developing the character and integrity needed to fulfill that role. To truly become a king after God's own heart (1 Samuel 13:14), it was crucial for David to receive the prophecy from God, which became instrumental in mentoring, guarding, and developing David through the wilderness years before he assumed the role of king.

I believe there will be times when God wants us to focus on one area of our life, "this one thing I do" (Philippians 3:13). Instead of attempting to spiritually multitask, we should allow God to work in the specific areas He desires to address in this season. We will navigate through them according to God's timing and plan, successfully transitioning into the next season.

We have included below a list of 10 foundational spiritual disciplines that we believe every Christian should engage in. I encourage you to think about these in two ways:

1. Spend some time with God, thinking and writing down an overall vision of how you wish to live in this area of your life for the rest of your life.

2. Look at your life in small time frames, think and work through what the habits would be of a person who was living that life. How can you practically work this into the fabric of your daily life?

I. PRAYER

Prayer is the heartbeat of God. Prayer is communicating with God. As believers, we should envision ourselves as individuals who live lives steeped in prayer. We are called to be people of faith in our prayers, believing in the promises of God. We believe that when we pray, heaven responds to our petitions. We pray diligently, enjoying prayer as a sustaining part of our lives. Our vision includes praying in three primary ways:

1. An ongoing walk of prayer: We desire for prayer, communication with God, and fellowship with the Lord to permeate every aspect of our lives. Smith Wigglesworth once said, "I never pray more than 15 minutes, but I never go more than 15 minutes without praying." Our vision is to have a prayer life that is continuous and integrated into our daily existence.

2. Specific times of dedicated prayer: We aim to set aside specific times when we set the world aside and commune with

our God. Having a morning routine where God is the sole focus of our being is a valuable daily discipline. We envision dedicating time each day to pray for specific things, ensuring our connection with heaven remains consistent.

3. Corporate prayer: We commit to being individuals who gather with others to pray collectively. We recognize that corporate prayer is an integral part of the spiritual life.

II. BIBLE READING

"Man shall not live by bread alone, but by every word which proceeds from the mouth of God." Matthew 4:4

When we read the Word of God, we are fellowshipping with God. When we read the Bible, we are hearing the voice of God. Jesus said, "The words that I speak to you are spirit, and they are life." John 6:63.

It is vital for every Christian to engage with the Word of God in three primary ways:

Firstly, we need to read the Word of God. We all need a daily discipline of reading through the Bible, all of God's Word, allowing it to shape, inform, challenge, and wash us. "That He might sanctify and cleanse it with the washing of water by the Word." Ephesians 5:26

Secondly, we all need to learn the disciplines of engaging with specific Bible verses and portions. We need to grow in confessing the Word of God, memorize the Bible, and quote the Word of God to our own hearts (and also to Satan when he attacks us). We need to learn to be the prophet over our own life and be the one who will speak God's Word, that will change and shape the situations of our lives.

Thirdly, we all need to develop a corporate relationship with the Word of God. It is vital to be part of a local church where we participate collectively in the teaching of God's Word. As we grow as believers, we all should also engage in instructing others in God's Word.

III. SHARING YOUR FAITH

Every Christian is called to share his faith and pass the gospel along to others. Paul said to Timothy, "And the things that you have heard from me among many witnesses, commit these to faithful men who will be able to teach others also." 2 Timothy 2:2

Every believer should learn to share his faith in two primary ways:

Intentionally. These are the times when we should actively approach others and seek to share the gospel with them. The more we develop this into a personal discipline, the less fear of man will sway in our hearts. We need to practice this and learn to rely on the leading and guiding of the Spirit in this manner.

Secondly, we need to learn to give witness to the veracity of the gospel in a natural and unconscious way. We should all live our lives in a way that we communicate the reality of Jesus to those around us even without specifically trying. Charles Spurgeon said, "Share the gospel with those around you, and if necessary, use words." Our lives should carry power and give witness to the living God inside us.

IV. SILENCE

Silence should play an important role in the life of the believer. We live in a world of noise, chatter, and distraction. The world around us is constantly trying to fill our lives with things that will take the place of God in our focus and affections. There is something vitally important in learning the spiritual discipline of practicing silence before the Lord.

"Surely I have calmed and quieted my soul, like a weaned child with his mother." Psalm 131:2

There is an important aspect of faith involved in silence. When we live a Christian life where we are constantly doing something, saying something, engaging in spiritual activities, etc., we can often hide behind those things. When we are still before the Lord, we actually develop our vital connection with Him.

V. FASTING

There is incredible power in the spiritual discipline of fasting. When Jesus taught about fasting, he used the phrase "when you fast," not "if you fast" (Matthew 6:16). Fasting is basically the act of abstaining. We usually associate fasting with the concept of abstaining from food, but it could also be applied to many other areas of life (entertainment, technology, things we enjoy, relationships, etc.). It is very important that we do not approach fasting with a religious mindset. As we have said earlier, the danger is that somebody will look at fasting through the grid of thinking that if I am suffering, then God will reward me.

Fasting is not about being hungry. Fasting is about experiencing hunger and then bringing that hunger to God instead of relying on natural resources. Fasting is about feeding oneself and drawing life and energy from the spirit instead of from the natural man. When we do this, there is incredible power released in fasting. Fasting does not change God. "For I am the Lord, I do not change" (Malachi 3:6). Rather, fasting changes ourselves. We need to learn to fast by faith and believe that this is working based on the promises of God, not on our feelings. Probably the worst time in the world to judge something by your feelings is when you are fasting.

VI. GIVING/GENEROSITY

Every Christian has been called to give. Giving should not be regarded as an action we perform; rather, a giver should be an identity we embrace for the rest of our lives. "For God so loved the world that He gave His only begotten Son" (John 3:16). I believe every Christian should commit to the discipline of giving as the Bible commands us to. Without a commitment, we will tend to give based on our emotions, which means we will often refrain from giving.

I believe every Christian should be involved in giving at four different levels:

* * *

1. TITHES

Tithing is a principle that predates the law, continues through the law, and persists after the law. Hebrews seven states that under the law, tithes were presented to the priest, but now as new covenant believers, we present our tithes directly to Jesus. (Hebrews 7:8) To tithe basically means to give the first portion, which the Bible defines as the first 10% of your actual income, and dedicate that to the work of God, specifically to the place where you are spiritually nourished.

2. OFFERINGS

Offerings are not based on a defined amount in scripture but on the leading of the Holy Spirit, or the generosity of the believer's heart. An offering could be a gift to a person or a church organization that might occur in an occasional manner, as opposed to a regular tithe. We should all be led by the Holy Spirit in the way that we give offerings.

3. GIVING THAT THE GOSPEL WOULD GO FORTH TO THE NATIONS

I believe that it is the role of every believer to give that the gospel would go forth to the nations. We should be led by the Spirit in the way in which we do this. Personally, I think that everybody should be partnering with an organization or ministry that is sharing the gospel with those who have not yet met Jesus.

4. GIVING TO THE POOR

Finally, the Bible encourages every believer to give to the

poor. In one sense, Jesus is clear that the poor will always be with us. We will never eliminate poverty from the Earth through our giving. Yet, the Lord calls us to give to our neighbors, to those we meet who are suffering and in need. The poor might not always be those whom we would necessarily define as poor. We need to be led by the Holy Spirit in the way and manner in which we do this.

VII. CELEBRATION & JOY

We may not traditionally think of celebration or joy as a discipline, but I believe it is vital that we do so.

It is important for us to regard joy and celebration as something we need to commit to. We need joy. "The joy of the Lord is our strength" (Nehemiah 8:10). If we simply rejoice when we feel like rejoicing, joy will not become a prominent part of our life.

It is interesting to note that when the Bible exhorts us to be joyful and rejoice, this is seen as a commandment and not something that will automatically happen. There is something powerful about the discipline of gathering with other Christians and rejoicing and celebrating in the goodness of our God. We often do not initially feel like doing this, and yet, when we do, we will feel like it. I encourage you to develop the habits, the daily disciplines, and the glorious work of celebrating God and enjoying Him. Our chief purpose in life is to enjoy God, not to keep commandments. When we enjoy God, we will naturally keep His commandments.

VIII. SACRIFICE

There are some aspects of disciplines that we eagerly embrace and enjoy. The concept of sacrifice is not something that comes easily to most of us, particularly in the modern Western cultural setting. And yet, in spite of that, God calls us to live a life of sacrifice.

In John 12, Jesus teaches the disciples that unless a grain of corn falls into the ground and dies, it must abide alone, but if it dies, it will bring forth much fruit. (John 12:24) I believe there is a legitimate sacrifice that all of us are called to make for the sake of the gospel. What can be difficult is discerning between the suffering that God allows, and the areas of suffering in life that He does not desire for us.

There are seven different categories of suffering that we will all go through as Christians. The key is to recognize the source of this suffering and then to recognize the antidote or answer to that situation:

1. Satan
2. Ourselves
3. Other people
4. A fallen world
5. A lack of knowledge
6. Suffering for the sake of the gospel
7. The bridegroom suffering paradigm

1. Satan is real, and so is the demonic realm. There is suffering that will come to us because of Satan. The antidote to

this is to take authority over him in our lives. If we passively submit to suffering that Satan brings, we are not walking in our authority.

2. We suffer because of ourselves. Often in life, we suffer because of the poor or sinful choices that we have made. We cannot blame Satan or other people. The antidote to this is to repent of the errors and mistakes we have made in the past, and to ask God for wisdom and grace to change those things within our lives.

3. We will all suffer because of other people. Some of this suffering is legitimate. There are times when God wants us to help others and we pay a price in doing that. Other times, this suffering is not legitimate, and we simply need to distance ourselves from people who will cause unnecessary suffering in our lives.

4. We will all suffer because we live in a fallen world, one that is not subject to the perfection of God. We live in a world that is subjugated to sin and the curse. At times in our lives, all of us will suffer because we live in the world in which the creation groans for the manifestation of the sons of God (Romans 8:19). The antidote to this is to believe God by faith for protection from that suffering, but also to realize that this world is not our home. We seek a city whose builder and maker is God (Hebrews 11:10), and our hope is not in the redemption of this world but in the future kingdom where the lion will lie down with the lamb.

5. One of the chief areas of suffering in the life of a Christian is because of a lack of knowledge. "My people suffer for a lack of knowledge" (Hosea 4:6). Often, Christians think they are

suffering in a legitimate form of persecution when simply they do not know God's word. This is why Jesus said, "You will know the truth, and the truth will set you free" (John 8:32). Christians are suffering because they simply do not know the truth of God's word and His promises. The antidote to this suffering is to spend time in God's word.

6. We all will, or should, suffer persecution for righteousness' sake. There is legitimate persecution that will come into the life of the believer as we lay down our lives to share the gospel both with those around us and the nations. This is the primary suffering that is read about in the New Testament. It is not suffering because of our own foolishness or that of others but rather because Satan hates the propagation of the gospel. It is important to realize that as we suffer for the gospel's sake, grace is available to us. This is the suffering that Paul described when he taught about his thorn in the flesh (2 Corinthians 12:7).

7. Lastly, there is a strange suffering that can sound counterintuitive. This is the suffering we will experience when we get a glimpse of who Jesus is. This is what I would call the bridal suffering. Jesus said when the bridegroom is with the bride, they do not fast, but the day will come when the bridegroom is taken away. (Matthew 9:15) The apostle Paul said, "We who were in this tabernacle do groan" (2 Corinthians 5:4). There is legitimate suffering that we should embrace in our lives because we long to be set free from this fallen world and yearn to live in the presence of our Lord. This suffering will drive us to fasting and to seeking God. It is painful, and yet glorious.

IX. PERSONAL WORSHIP

God calls us to worship. Our primary identity is as worshipers. When we worship, we are connected with God and glory and intimacy. For many believers, the first and only relationship with worship is in a corporate worship setting. Worshiping with other believers is a glorious and indeed necessary thing, and yet there is something incredibly powerful about learning to worship when nobody sees you except your Father, who is in heaven. In the same way as Jesus spoke about during the sermon on the mount about giving in secret, praying in secret, etc. He said that "your Father, who sees in secret will reward you openly." (Matthew 6:6)

I believe that every Christian should learn the discipline of worshiping when nobody else is looking. We should learn to worship without other people helping, without a worship band, or a stage or light show. If we want to go deeper in God, then we must develop the daily discipline of worshiping God because He is worthy and finding joy in His presence. (John 4:23)

X. MEDITATION

Meditation is often regarded as the process of emptying one's mind of all conscious thought. True meditation, Bible meditation, is the absolute opposite concept. So much of the current ideas of meditation are actually dangerous and connected to Satanism and witchcraft. When you try to empty your mind of all conscious thoughts, then Satan will fill it. Rather, biblical meditation is the process of filling our minds with the thoughts of God. God wants us to take His thoughts and engage our mind with them until our hearts and passions are stirred with the things of heaven. We are transformed by the renewing of our mind. (Romans 12:2) This involves the biblical practice of meditation.

We can choose the contents of our mind when we become intentional and embrace the biblical discipline of meditation. (Isaiah 26:3)

"Whatever things are good, pure, lovely, virtuous, think on these things" (Philippians 4:8).

We should follow the example of Mary, the mother of Jesus. When Mary received prophetic words from Gabriel, Zachariah, Elizabeth, and others, the Bible says she stored these things up in her heart and pondered them (Luke 2:19). We can learn to practice thinking upon the things of God. It is vital that this becomes part of a daily discipline, and that we choose times to do this with intentionality. If we do not choose what we play upon the screen of our minds, then the world, the flesh, and the devil will.

As you build a personal vision statement for this area of your life, I encourage you to pray that the Lord would show you the daily disciplines he would have you focus on in this season. Sometimes we need to add new disciplines into our day. Other times we need to reinforce those we may have neglected. There are times of upgrade where God wants to take a discipline into a new level in our lives.

Questions for Meditation

- *Are there ideas and scripts about this area of your life that heaven wants to rewrite in this season?*

- *What are the challenges you have in relation to this subject? Describe them as past, defeated, and nailed to the cross.*

- *What is the Lord displacing in your life? What new thing does He want to replace the old with?*

- *How does God define my identity?*

- *Describe the relationship that God is calling you to have with Him in this area.*

- *If God were saying "Yes and Amen", what would your request be?*

- *What would living in complete freedom, joy, and victory look like?*

- *What promise is God speaking over you in this season? What are the promises He is calling you to declare back to Him?*

- *What would transformation look like under your present circumstances?*

- *What would it take for you to develop a mindset, a lifestyle, a persona of fullness as a way of life?*

- *How are you called to minister to others?*

Chapter Thirteen

The Vision Filled Life

God has a vision for your life. The aim of this book is to challenge you to write down God's vision and how He wishes you to walk before Him. As previously mentioned, there is power in transitioning from a vague sense of how God would have you live to a specific written vision. Vision fills our hearts with passion. Writing a vision is an act of faith. A vision is an invitation from heaven to step into a future defined by Father God.

I encourage you to take the questions at the end of each chapter and present them before the Lord in prayer. Write down the things that stir your heart. Do not attempt to discriminate or triage these thoughts too much. Allow the Holy Spirit to flow ideas and images into your heart. Ask Him to give you scriptures that become personal words to you. This is a journey, this is a process, and one that will never be completely finished until you see the ultimate vision of Jesus face to face. As you work through this process, do not simply endeavor to define actions or situations... "I will do this," "I will accomplish" this, etc. Rather, focus on your identity in Christ and on the relationship with Father God that you are being called to.

* * *

God called Moses to "Come up the mountain, and Be there" (Exodus 24:12). Your call is to be, not to do. Your actions will flow from your identity.

How do we use this vision as part of our ongoing walk with God?

"Write the vision
And make it plain on tablets,
That he may run who reads it."
Habakkuk 2:2

Learn to return to this vision each day and hear God speaking it to you. As we walk through our normal lives, we are all influenced (in more ways than we know) by the world around us. When we see God's vision, we are cleansed from the lens of the world. Our hearts are recalibrated to heaven's reality.

Set your mind on things above, not on things on the earth. For you died, and your life is hidden with Christ in God. When Christ who is our life appears, then you also will appear with Him in glory. (Colossians 3:2)

The purpose of a vision is to see that vision. God has said something, so that you may see something. Take the time to read through that vision and allow your heart to be realigned with the heart of God each day. When we see Jesus, we will become like him. (1 John 3:2). This is primarily spoken of the return of the Lord, but it is equally true today. To the extent that we see Jesus, to that extent, will we be like Him right now.

Do not view your vision through the lens of your own

abilities and capacities. God will give you a vision that has nothing to do with your abilities and everything to do with His power, grace, and resources.

"Son of man, look with your eyes and hear with your ears, and fix your mind on everything I show you; for you were brought here so that I might show them to you. Declare to the house of Israel everything you see."
Ezekiel 40:4.

Look with your eyes
Hear with your ears
Set your heart upon these things
Go and declare them.

Lastly, we encourage you to declare this vision loudly over your life. Do not rush from conference to conference seeking a prophecy for your life. Become the prophet over your own life and speak God's vision. When you do so, you will see your world change, and in turn, change the world around you.

Selah

Graham Jones Ministries

Originally from England, Evangelist Graham Jones divides his time between ministry in Europe and the USA. Graham's heart is and passion is revival and seeing the presence and power of God released back into the church. Graham speaks in churches, conferences, universities, and businesses in many different countries each year. He brings a breath of fresh air and passion to God's people as he encourages them to come back to simple supernatural Christianity.

Graham is used particularly in the area of physical healing and has seen many people healed from all manner of sickness through simple faith in God's promises and the manifest presence of God. Graham is one of the only people ever invited to preach inside the United Nations in New York City resulting in many giving their lives to Jesus and people healed in the UN building.

In 2012 after 10 years of missionary work in France, Graham moved his ministry base to the New England area of the USA. Graham believes he has a mandate to stir revival in local churches and help bring another great awakening in the USA. He is currently working with local churches of many different denominations holding 1-3 day events aimed at releasing revival in the church and touching the surrounding communities.

Graham is involved in missions and church planting. He oversees churches in Europe, India, and North America. GJM works through relationships with local churches, seeking both to reach the world and equip the church with teaching seminars where believers are practically taught to move in the gifts of the Spirit and believe God to heal people. GJM works to see local churches moving in revival and the freedom of the Holy Spirit.

Graham and his wife Léa have a missions base in the town of St Etienne in the south of France. Graham has been an ordained minister with IGO (International Gospel Outreach) in the UK for many years.

Graham read theology at the L'EBZ Institute in Paris, France.

Made in the USA
Middletown, DE
24 August 2024

59121445R00135